HISTORY'S CHOICE

Other Books by Irena Narell

Ashes to the Taste
A Study of Polish Communism, 1961

The Invisible Passage
Short Story Collection, 1969

Joshua, Fighter for Bar Kochba, 1978
Young Adult Novel

Our City, The Jews of San Francisco, 1981
From the Gold Rush to the Present

HISTORY'S CHOICE

A Writer's Journey From Poland to America

Irena Narell

Akiba Press
Oakland, California

Cover design by Donna Mendes-Visco
Front cover photo: author's collection
Back cover photo by Steve Visco

Manufactured in the United States of America

Akiba Press
P.O. Box 13086
Oakland, CA 94661

───────────────────────────

Publisher's Cataloging-in-Publication
(Prepared by Quality Books Inc.)

Narell, Irena.
    History's choice : a writer's journey from Poland to America /
Irena Narell
        p.   cm.
        LCCN: 95-078186
        ISBN 0-934764-03-4
        1. Narell, Irena.   I. Title

CT275.N37 1995   920
                                                    QBI95-20328

Contents

For my father and my husband—
My beloved spirits

Preface

There is no time I can recall when I did not wish to be a writer. Literature has been the beacon and meaning of my life. Writing has cost me a great deal of effort and an almost equal amount of disappointment and pain. It has also brought me some recognition, accompanied by a measure of success. Nonetheless, the price one has to pay for doing meaningful and compassionate work has often been so high that periodically I abandoned my quest. No matter how many of one's books have been published, praised, and liked, approaching a publisher with a new work is still problematic, and rejection just as unpleasant. I often availed myself of any excuse to get away from writing.

For a few years I worked for the Polish Delegation to the United Nations. Disillusionment with "socialist" Poland followed my home leave in the country of my birth. I got married while still a college student, and had one son. I wrote my study of Polish communism *Ashes to the Taste,* (New York: University Publishers, 1961), shortly after my second son was born.

My abiding interest in art resulted in my opening an art gallery with a friend. This consumed several years of my time, keeping me safely away from writing. I acquired a considerable art collection, however, since I became my own best client. Later, my sons' successful musical group took up an even greater amount of my time. But still, during that period I wrote a young-adult novel, *Joshua, Fighter for Bar Kochba,* about an ancient revolt of the Jews against Rome, and some short stories. I was always encouraged by my wonderful literary agent, Mary Squire Abbot of McIntosh and Otis, who believed in my talent— often more than I did myself. She was the second admirable woman in my life to encourage me in a writing career. The first was my English professor at Columbia University, Dr. Dorothy Brewster, my beloved teacher and dear friend. Both are now gone, and I miss them.

Following our move to California in 1970 I became fascinated with the gold rush period and the role that pioneer Jews played in the early history of the state. I spent years in research libraries and in interviewing pioneer descendants, gathering materials from families, major libraries, and collections of Victorian photographs.

I wrote and published a number of articles on this subject, and also saw the publication in 1978 of *Joshua*—it received the 1979 National Jewish Book Award—and of *OUR CITY: the Jews of San Francisco,* in

1981. The promotion of these books again took years away from writing. When I finally got ready for another book, this time about my unique Polish childhood, I became involved with a photographic and oral history project instead. That took four more years and a good deal of effort to complete. In 1986 I discovered that a prominent author of potboilers had copied three of her chapters from *OUR CITY*, word for word. Copyright lawyers advised me to sue, which I did, and was offered a settlement of $12,500 by the author—which I deemed wholly inadequate, in view of her multimillion dollar contract. With the help of an insurance policy against plagiarism, her publishers then launched a counteroffensive through a major San Francisco law firm, spending more than $250,000 on the case. They found a judge who did not understand copyright law, and the case never came to trial. I spent two years helping my attorney prepare our case, but we were overwhelmed by the weight of my opponent's financial resources.

Then fate intervened in a tragic way. I lost my wonderful and supportive husband to lymphatic cancer. An extremely healthy and athletic man, he shocked us all by succumbing to this dreadful disease. My grief was overwhelming. I was paralyzed—I could neither read nor write. More than a year elapsed before I could face the world again and contemplate whether I wanted to go on living and writing. I have only recently returned to working on the memoir of my Polish childhood.

My books are here for everyone to see, but my essays and short stories have been scattered among many publications—in story collections, books of essays, and magazines. My idea of having them all together, with some miscellany, has come to fruition in this volume. Peter Browning, my friend and colleague from the Institute for Historical Study, has worked very hard to make this book possible. I thank him for his patience and editing skills.

The pieces in this volume are not all in chronological order. Sometimes an earlier piece and a much later one are together so that the reader can follow the evolution of the writer's feelings and ideas. This is true of "Son of Poland" and "My Uncles Judah and Benzion," and of two short stories, "The Invisible Passage" and "A Room Not One's Own." The short story "Syngar the Slave" has since become a young-adult novel with an acceptable 'happy' ending.

My numerous essays on California's pioneer Jews are not included here. They require a volume of their own. My lectures on various facets of Jewish history, ancient and contemporary, also belong to another time and place.

IRENA NARELL

Politics and Family

Son of Poland

The letter came back today. I weighed the envelope in my hands; it looked shabby and a little worn out from the long journey. The stamp on its back said: "Addressee cannot be found." The words had a familiar sound.

In 1935 the letter from the concentration camp came back this way.

In 1938 the letter from Prague came back just like that.

I keep wondering where you are now, just as I did all those times, marked by all those returned letters, and now, just as in the times before this one, I can't find the answer. I don't know whether it's wise even to think about you, because when I do I have to give way to the old fear and the old uncertainty. We thought you were safe at last, we thought the adventures of your twenty-eight years had finally come to a close, we thought you had found a place in which to rest.

I said goodbye to you six years ago, and it seems as if it were only yesterday. I've become a young woman since then; you—a weary fighter for the rights of man. I've wanted to talk to you a thousand times during all those years, I wanted you to help me to destroy thousands of doubts. I needed your many years of fighting, but I couldn't reach you and so I grew up all by myself. And I haven't done an awfully good job of it, I'm afraid. I don't even know whether you would give me your approval. Because all I could say to you now, if you could hear me, would be: Janek, I'm not sure where I am, and I'm not sure where I am going, and there is just one thing that I *am* certain of: I will never give up our ideals for the peaceful fireplace and self-satisfied existence of the middle class. That much I can promise you, but only that much.

Six years ago you walked out of the house with two policemen at you side, your tall figure towering above them; you turned around to look at me, smiled, and never came back. I had seen you go so many times before that I could even hold back the tears. So that "they" wouldn't see one of us broken, I raised my fist, and with all the power of a little girl's heart I promised never to forget that day. The door closed with an ominous sound. It was closing on our whole past, only we didn't know it—none of us, Mother, Dad, or I. My mother's little brother had left for good. Our world was slipping from our fingers, the thunder of invading armies was sounding its first alarm on our doorstep, but we were deaf and blind.

Janek was always the kind of boy who "would give you the shirt off his back." He was constantly broke, and constantly in trouble with his elders. He was well-liked by young people, and usually got unexpected favors from all of them.

Janek liked our house better than he did his own, and would go to grandfather's only to sleep or pick up some of his books. When I was little, he used to spend most of his time with me. When I grew up and could really appreciate him, he wasn't there any longer.

I always associate Janek with wonderful times, funny stories, songs, and furry animals. It was he who brought me my first dog and taught me to love him. It was he who picked up a homeless little cat and brought him home.

He scolded me for pulling the cat's tail, and he taught me the little game of tolerance. I can still see him on winter nights in front of the fire, his long legs stretched before him, the dog on one side, the cat on the other, both watching him with loving eyes. I can hear his voice as he told me tall tales of imaginary adventures or funny stories I adored. I could never imagine his going away from that fire, and leaving us behind—the dog, the cat, and me.

The first time I missed his cheerful voice and jokes I asked Mother why he didn't come, and just then noticed that she had been crying. Janek was supposed to take his final examination in the Gymnasium three weeks from that day, and I knew he had to study, but why didn't he come anyway? She took my hand, and said, "Darling, Janek's been arrested, I don't think he will have to take his exam now." It was so difficult to understand. How could anyone arrest a boy who went around picking up homeless dogs and cats, who gave the last cent of his allowance to old janitor Peter, who let his little niece walk all over him, who was always there when you needed him. Couldn't they see they were making a terrible mistake?

Finally Daddy explained it all to me. Janek wanted everyone to have an equal chance. It seemed that he wanted the world to give Peter and others like him enough work and enough food. Daddy himself believed in the same thing. But Janek wanted the change to come as soon as possible, so he joined the Communist Party, which in our country was illegal. He was caught and put in prison.

Shortly afterwards Janek was released, took his final exam, and grandfather, already worried, sent him to the University of Cracow, where his other son was teaching. That was our first goodbye. No more evenings in front of the fire, no more stories, no more songs. I would talk to my animals about him—they understood. And we would all wait patiently for Christmas and summer vacations when our long-legged boy would come back with hundreds of new stories and new games.

Early one morning Daddy woke me up and said that Janek was brought home from college by the police the night before. He said he knew I was a brave little girl and wouldn't tell Mother until he found out what it was all about. I didn't tell Mother. I said to my dog, and to Kiza, the cat, that after all, we could take it better than she would, and even if we loved him we could stand a little worry and a little pain.

It all turned out to be one big worry and one great pain. I can still remember waiting for the trial to end, the dragging hours, the final blow. Mother staggered under it; grandfather added many a gray hair because of it; I couldn't even cry. Five years' imprisonment for Communist activity at the university.

I went to see him in prison and took him chocolate. He was peaceful and full of joy, as he had always been; he never let us see how he really felt. Only when we had said goodbye and turned toward the gate, I glanced over my shoulder—the prison guard was showing him the way back—and there was such a look of longing and utter sadness in his eyes that I could hardly keep from crying out loud: "Let him out, will you! Let him out!"

In a few weeks he was sent to one of the most notorious prisons in the country, almost a thousand kilometers from home. I couldn't visit him any longer.

We wrote to him often. He always asked for books, more and more books, more and more newspapers and magazines. And whenever a prisoner came out from behind the stone walls we would get a long letter, uncensored and painstakingly printed on large, thin sheets of paper, delivered to us at great risk by the departing prisoner, and giving us the real truth about Janek's life there. He was able to organize all the political prisoners into a strong group; they had means of communication; they studied together; and together they waited.

After two and a half years an amnesty for political prisoners was declared, and Janek came home. He was still very young and he was still the same. The prison cell hadn't broken his integrity; it hadn't taken away any of his dignity, his ideals, his charm. But he came back very sick, with tubercular lungs, and not very much time to live.

We sent Janek to the white mountains of Poland, to the fresh icy air, to help cure his bleeding lungs—we had to smile and wave him goodbye once more. And when he came back in the spring he was better, and could give me a whole lecture on being too much under Dad's influence, and even succeeded in winning me over to his side. I told Dad with a somewhat guilty expression that his philosophy was all wrong—that it was outdated.

The police came just before the first of May and took him. It had become a habit for them to arrest Janek, and he was the first person on the lists of their yearly spring arrests. He was taken to one of the overcrowded prisons of Lvov, and we lost track of him completely. Then a rumor spread. Someone said that Janek was in the newly formed concentration camp at Bereza Kartuska, one of the most dreadful places in Europe. The letter we wrote came back, but two months later a little postcard in Janek's handwriting came in the morning's mail, stamped "Bereza Kartuska Isolation Camp" on the side.

One day a prisoner returned home. An old friend of Janek's, he came back a changed man, with a broken body and unstable mind. And from him we learned of a little slip of paper that was offered to all the prisoners at the camp; if they would sign it, they would be set free. It didn't say much, it just took away all one's rights as a human being, his right to do as he pleased, his right to think and believe as he saw fit. *"I swear that I will never engage in any political activity, I swear that I will report my every step to the police, I swear . . . ."* I swear my life away.

"The boy hasn't any sense," his friend told us. "Me? I jumped at the opportunity and signed it, but your boy, he just refused point blank." He couldn't have signed that slip of paper, I said—can't you understand?

In the evening of a February day the doorbell rang, and my dog ran to the door, furiously wagging his tail. He waited impatiently for me with dancing eyes. "What are you making a fool of yourself for?" I said. "You know you're the meanest dog in this town, and you don't give a hoot for any of my friends." But he knew better. Because I opened the door to a tall, familiar figure in a long trench coat, and somebody's long arms were about me before I could speak. The dog was crying with joy. I couldn't say a word. Janek was back, and I couldn't believe it.

We were so happy to have him back. We asked no questions, but we got our answer soon. The boy was still our Janek. But there wasn't as much of a boy left in him as there was of a man who had seen suffering, and lots of it. He would talk to me for long hours about the men who stayed behind. After a while I got a complete picture of the concentration camp, and tried to remember it, even if it hurt. I shall remember it so long as there is any life left in my body; I shall remember the tortures, the blood, the murder of that camp.

His education was over. No university would accept a boy with Janek's kind of a past; no one would give him a job. He used to pace up and down my room, his long legs covering almost half of its length at a step, a frown on his forehead, silent—for hours. I would try to talk to him, but I knew what bothered my friend, and I also knew that I could not help him. Janek went away before the spring. The police were looking for victims, and he had become such a habit with them that, active or not, he would be suspected and jailed.

Grandfather couldn't take it. He died of heart failure on Easter Day. Both his sons came to the funeral—the university professor, a famous man, and the boy with a broken life and shining eyes. The boy seemed very moved, and at the cemetery told Dad and me that he would be home a little later; besides, he thought the police were already looking for him.

They were. They were waiting for him at our house when we came back. The commandant himself, three secret policemen, and two in uniform had all come for our dangerous criminal. But we came back without Janek, and so they left. The doorbell rang soon afterwards, and our hunted boy came in, breathless. Mother gave him some dinner, his professor brother, Dad, and I watched him silently, his curly head bent over the plate of hot soup, his lips set firmly in a narrow line. And just as silently we waited for the inevitable. The doorbell again. The loud shuffling of feet. Again they took him away.

It was raining hard that night; I can still remember it. The telephone rang. It was the commandant, and would we please pack up some things for young Mr. K.? I put down the receiver with shaking hands. Janek was taking a trip again.

Dad went over to the police station to talk to him. And Janek had said, "They're sending me back to the concentration camp. It's easier than putting me on trial here—they don't have to prove anything. And this time, I am not coming back." Dad came home soon afterwards. Mother packed a bag. We didn't speak. And suddenly, the doorbell rang again. We were so used to doorbells that brought bad news and secret policemen by then that we weren't even startled out of our silence. I went to the door and saw before me two breathless boys, old friends of mine, who whispered, "Janek escaped from the police station a few minutes ago!"—and they disappeared.

The police were out looking for him far into the night. I could picture him, running through that violent rain, coatless, feverish, and haunted. I fell asleep crying.

We heard from him a few days later. The good people of a neighboring village sheltered him and shared their food with him. Then Mother went to a border town, a friend drove Janek there in his car (all that at a risk of ten to fifteen years imprisonment for helping an escaped prisoner), an experienced guide took him over the "green border" despite the many guards, and he was in free Czechoslovakia.

And Czechoslovakia gave him what his own country had refused. It gave him political freedom and a chance to study. But the great clouds were already gathering over Europe. Before long German troops occupied Czechoslovakia, and the letter we wrote to Janek came back, unanswered and unopened. Strangely enough, Janek was back with us in Poland, only we didn't know it, and neither did the police. Poland, ironically, was the only avenue of escape from Hitler. On a little fisherman's boat Janek and a few others undertook the dangerous journey across the Baltic Sea to England.

Janek wrote his most beautiful letters from England. He told us about the fall of Czechoslovakia, and he told us how well the British treated Czech refugees, because they were already beginning to be ashamed of Munich. And after Poland fell, he told us of the old bureaucracy prevailing in the offices of the government-in-exile, of the fat gentlemen sitting behind the desks, of their old narrowness and inefficiency, and the familiar red tape. His lungs were bothering him again; the long flight in the rain had left its scars. But he could not stand inactivity for long, and he took a job in one of the defense factories, a job as a carrier, the hardest of its kind, but the only one offered to a foreigner. In the midst of it all he managed to marry a young Russian doctor whom he had met in Prague several months earlier.

The last I heard he was going to join the army to fight for what he had believed in for so long, though with his tubercular lungs I don't know how they could have accepted him. He said to me in his last letter: "The increased efforts of those who want to break us should fill you with new hope. They simply mean that we are growing stronger."

I have not heard from him since that letter. My own was returned. But I believe in the day that will announce the Allied victory, the day that will bring Janek back to us in a free and independent people's Poland.

"Son of Poland" was the expression of an idealistic (and deluded) young girl. It was published in New Masses, the U.S. Communist Party's prestigious literary magazine (now defunct). It was my first published work. I was not yet an American citizen, and I used the pseudonym Eve Grot. In my own defense as a radical let me quote Arthur Koestler: "There is a world of difference between a disappointed lover and one incapable of love."

My Uncles Judah and Benzion

A Personal Memoir

We are a small East European Jewish family, further decimated by the hellfires of this century. Yet even for us, accustomed as we are to loss, the last few years have been heavily burdened with three deaths. One was that of my mother, an old lady, ill and worn with suffering; the others were her brothers. They were Dr. Benzion Katz, pen name Benzion Benshalom, classical scholar, Hebrew poet, two terms the Rector of Tel Aviv University, a devoted servant of Israel, and Juliusz (born Judah) Katz-Suchy, Minister Extraordinary and Plenipotentiary, Permanent Representative of Poland to the United Nations, Ambassador to India, professor at Warsaw's Institute of Political Science, in effect a servant of the Soviet Union. In the complete divergence of their lives, the two men personified the opposing forces that rent Jewish intellectual life during their youth—and to some extent continue to do so today.

Their birthplace and mine was Sanok, the district's capital, a small town in the Carpathian Mountains of Poland. Sanok boasted a courthouse, library, movie theatre, several secondary schools—and a population almost fifty per cent Jewish. The Jewish community was divided into "ghetto" Jews, mainly peddlers and shopkeepers, and the emancipated professionals, such as lawyers, physicians, and dentists. Several generations had lived under the rule of the Hapsburgs in the portion of annexed Polish territory known as Galicia. Following World War I, Poland became a republic. Marshal Pilsudski's 1926 coup d'etat effectively concluded its short-lived attempt at parliamentary democracy.

Like other Jewish households, ours mirrored the political ferment that had jolted Jewish society from its intellectual isolation. No sooner had Jews emerged from the confines of a religious past to face the modern dilemmas of the twentieth century, than they plunged into the avant-garde of all its great socio-political movements. Our family represented no fewer than three. Socialism was personified by my father, a labor and criminal lawyer, a prominent figure in the Socialist party of pre-World War II Poland and a leader of the Bund. Zionism was the creed of my uncle Benzion, Communism that of my uncle Judah. Ironically, Judah arrived at communism via the leftwing Hashomer Hatzair, a Zionist youth group, while my uncle Benzion became a Zionist after participating in a Communist cell. However, both men considered themselves Socialists to the end of their lives.

Their grandfather was Judah Katz, a rabbi of considerable renown, whose family had lived in Sanok for several centuries. The only photograph taken of his keen face, long white beard, and majestic figure is preserved in family albums. This transgression of the holy law occurred while Rabbi Judah was vacationing in Carlsbad, where a photographer took his picture without his knowledge and exhibited it in a shop window. When the rabbi's only son, Sholom—Benzion and Judah's father—saw the photograph, he secretly bought all the existing copies and paid the photographer to destroy the negative. We also possess a Hebrew text by Rabbi Judah, published toward the end of his life and snatched from the jaws of the Holocaust. Entitled "The Call of Judah," it is a compilation of the religious and philosophical concepts underlying the Orthodox laws he administered. He had married well and owned considerable real estate in the town. His wife's family claimed, on I know not what authority, direct descent from King David.

After his death the family holdings rapidly dwindled, for Sholom had none of the rabbi's business acumen and was reduced to running a tobacco outlet, which was a government monopoly requiring a franchise. Eventually the political activities of Sholom's younger son, Judah—the rabbi's namesake—prompted the government to withdraw the franchise, leaving him with almost no income.

When I picture my grandfather, it is usually in that shop, his tall frame towering above the counter, his beard long since gone gray. Always there was the smell of tobacco about him, for he was an inveterate smoker despite a bout with nicotine poisoning that had cost him a leg. He walked a bit stiffly on a wooden limb, leaning heavily on a cane. Most of all, I remember his kindness.

On Saturdays my mother and I always went to Grandfather's for the midday meal, cooked the day before and kept warm in strict observance of the Sabbath. I came to these dinners late, straight from school, where a six-day week prevailed. Emulating my father, I was a militant atheist even at that early age, and would not cut classes on grounds of religious conviction. Thus week in and week out, carrying my schoolbooks, I desecrated my grandfather's Sabbath. In all those years of Saturdays, he never indicated by word or gesture that my disrespect for his beliefs caused him pain. Nor was there ever a word of reproach to his son-in-law, my father, or to Judah for their renunciation of religious tradition or their political affiliations. My grandfather's tolerance was especially remarkable because his view of the world was profoundly and completely Jewish. For him, as for generations past, the synagogue and the Law were the essence of life. Seen from that perspective, I can appreciate all the more the generosity of his silence.

Despite my disdain for what I considered outmoded Jewish practices, I enjoyed those Saturdays at Grandfather's. The walls were lined with Hebrew texts and German editions of Goethe, Schiller, Lessing, and Heine in gold-lettered leather bindings. The house was warm, quiet, and dignified, and the meal always delicious. After dinner, Grandfather would take a nap, leaving me with the latest issues of Polish magazines from his shop downstairs. Best of all were the rare occasions when Judah was home instead of in prison or in hiding. He would teach me forbidden revolutionary songs or talk about his experiences in the Communist underground—but always in whispers. There was an unspoken agreement that the peace of Grandfather's house would not be disturbed by political discussion. When both my uncles were in Sanok at the same time, they met at my father's house, where all three carried on heated political debates that remain among my childhood memories.

The Poland in which we lived was still primarily agricultural. Its emerging working class was oppressed, its peasantry illiterate and poverty-ridden. Factory owners resisted all attempts at unionization; the remnants of the aristocracy vacationed on the Mediterranean while the peasants went hungry. Pilsudski's one-party government had tolerated the existence of a large Jewish minority (3.5 million Jews in a population of almost 35 million) provided they were "good" Jews, loyal to the Marshal. After his death, in 1935, the ruling colonels openly sanctioned anti-Semitic outrages by the Nationalist party. There were bloody incidents among students at Polish universities, where a "ghetto bench" restriction was instituted by Nationalist students. This was followed by a campaign to boycott Jewish stores. In June 1936 Prime Minister Skladkowski officially approved the excesses with this statement: "My government considers that no one in Poland should be injured. An honest host does not allow anyone to be harmed in his house. But an economic fight, why not?" Six hundred years after King Casimir the Great had personally guaranteed Jewish settlement in Poland, we Jews were not only second-class citizens but "guests" in our country.

Then came other restrictive measures, ominous forerunners of the Nazi era. One required that first names be included on business and professional shingles, so that no Pole would unknowingly patronize a Jew. Another closed the bar to Jewish law school graduates, consigning them to lifetime clerkships.

Because they believed there was no future for Jews in Poland, Zionists such as Benzion felt that Jewish energies must be applied exclusively to the cause of a Jewish homeland. The Socialists, including the Jewish Socialist Bund, categorically rejected the Zionist solution. Since the colonels were anxious to rid Poland of Jews, the Socialists went so far as to hurl charges of "collaboration" against the Zionists. My father and Judah, for whom the government was the ultimate foe, thought that Zionism, with its counsel of eventual departure, would play directly into enemy hands. They supported the Socialist credo that Jews must stay in Poland and fight for a better life for all, and that, along with Poland's other economic and social problems, injustices against Jews would be eliminated only through the victory of Socialism.

By the middle and late 1930s both my young uncles had committed themselves irrevocably to their separate political paths. Benzion, though only in his mid-twenties, was gaining recognition as a Hebrew scholar. He had a doctorate in classical studies, had written his first book, and would soon occupy the chair in Hebrew studies established for him at the prestigious Jagiellonian University of Cracow. Professor Thaddeus Sinko, dean of Poland's philologists, advised baptism to assure Benzion a dazzling career, for in Poland, as in medieval Spain, this could open doors otherwise shut to Jews. He remained unbaptized, and married a young Zionist activist; there was no doubt that one day they would go to Palestine. Judah, like my father, had already been imprisoned more than once for his political convictions. His education had been permanently interrupted by expulsion from the university in 1932. Thus my grandfather had one son who brought him *naches* and one who created constant worry.

In February 1937 Judah returned home after nearly two years in the infamous Bereza Kartuska detention camp in Eastern Poland, where Communist Party members were incarcerated. He went to the mountains for a cure for incipient tuberculosis and then into hiding. When grandfather died that spring, Judah reappeared in Sanok for the funeral. The police were already looking for him; several hours later he was arrested in our house. I remember that it was raining, my mother was packing a bag to be taken to Judah, my father had gone to the police station to talk to the authorities, when suddenly the doorbell rang. Two young friends stood on the threshold. They whispered, "Judah escaped from the police station," and disappeared.

That night I fell asleep crying, as I pictured him making his way through the violent storm, coatless, feverish, and hunted. A few days later we heard from him. Later my mother made the difficult and dangerous arrangements—the risk was great, the penalties severe—to have him smuggled across the border of Czechoslovakia. There he lived, supported by my father, until that country was occupied by the Germans in 1938. He succeeded in fleeing through Poland and across the Baltic on a fisherman's boat to England, where he remained until the end of the war.

Viewed otherwise than through the eyes of an adoring child, Judah comes into even clearer focus in those early days. He had been the youngest and most indulged of three children. Though his mother died when he was ten, his older sister—my mother—took her place. He became the apple of her eye, more son than brother. After my mother married, my father took on the role of fairy godfather; invariably he handled Judah's emergencies and paid the bills. He also exerted great political influence on Judah, who wrote to me years later: "He had been more than a mere member of my family. Ideological ties bound me to him with greater force than family ties. Probably my whole conscious being is closely connected with his influence."

When, during his first year of law school, in 1932, Judah was arrested in Cracow for Communist activity, my father procured the services of one of Poland's most distinguished lawyers for his defense. Nevertheless, Judah was convicted, mainly because of his attempt to smuggle a letter out of jail. Throughout two and a half years of imprisonment in Lomza, near Warsaw, he sent a stream of requests for reading matter, and my father went to great trouble to supply him with a collection of modern Polish and European literature that a university would have been proud to own. On his release Judah, in typical fashion, left the books as a bequest to his fellow prisoners. When Judah was later in Bereza Kartuska, my father made herculean attempts to rescue him. At the outbreak of the war, when Judah was mistakenly arrested in London as an enemy alien, my father—stranded in New York without any resources—succeeded in obtaining his release.

My father and I had arrived in the United States in the summer of 1939 for a brief vacation. War broke out, and we found ourselves without a country. For a time my father struggled in the Polish émigré community, but it soon became clear that in these circles (no less than among ordinary Polish Americans) he was a double anathema as a Socialist and a Jew. Nor was he able to continue to be active in his beloved Jewish Bund, from which he eventually parted company on the issue of Soviet influence over Poland. In December 1945 he died suddenly, at fifty-one, barely a week before assuming his scheduled post as Poland's representative to the United Nations. In view of later developments within the Communist orbit, had he lived, he might have suffered a fate similar to that of his close friend, Jan Masaryk of Czechoslovakia.

A year later I went to work in the office of Oskar Lange at the Polish delegation to the United Nations. Though I was appalled at the high life-style of the new Poland's "people's representatives," I stayed on because of a rumor that Judah, formerly press attache at Poland's London Embassy, would soon join the delegation.

Though youthful illusions do not succumb easily, a good part of mine expired in the first encounter with my long-lost uncle. Eight years had elapsed since that rain-drenched flight from the Sanok police. I sought in vain for Judah Katz, the gallant figure from my past, the tall, slim, martyred fighter for the rights of man. Instead, I found Juliusz Katz-Suchy, a stout, balding, pompous official of the new Polish state who boasted of his medals and his exploits in attaining a prominent position in the party hierarchy. In addition to a new name (the "Suchy" amusingly meant "skinny," and was a holdover from underground days), he had also acquired considerable power—which he had used earlier in the Polish Foreign Ministry's passport division to throttle the efforts of others, including many Jews, to emigrate.

His undercover mission was to revamp the delegation along strict Communist party lines, for the Polish government was in the process of becoming a one-party system. Socialist Oskar Lange, a holdover from Poland's first provisional government of national unity, was removed. My uncle replaced him.

Katz-Suchy converted the delegation into a small dictatorship, introducing arbitrary working conditions and harsh disciplinary measures from which there was no appeal. He even employed a rudimentary spy system, though later the Polish government would provide more professional (security police) observers of its own. As a reward for his zeal, he was named Minister Extraordinary and Plenipotentiary. He moved to a Park Avenue penthouse where he did his diplomatic entertaining and kept scores of newspapermen supplied with food, ample drink, and funny stories. The once austere Communist became a connoisseur of luxury, preoccupied with accumulating material goods, and rationalizing the transformation as part of "having to keep up" with representatives of Western capitalist countries.

The only facet of my uncle's personality that had not undergone drastic change was his caustic humor, spiked with Yiddishisms. It was possible then to use Yiddish freely and casually, perhaps a reflection of the camaraderie which prevailed in the Polish Ministry of Foreign Affairs when its members were still predominantly Jewish. While many Jews in high places had, under party prodding, assumed Polish surnames, my uncle refused to do so.

Nevertheless he indulged in blatant hypocrisy, particularly when criticism of the Soviet Union was involved. Once my husband asked how representatives of a workers' state such as the Soviet Union, whose standard of living was still so low, could justify their expensive cars, clothes, and living quarters in the United States. The man who was known in diplomatic circles as a deflator of official pretensions accused my husband of having been victimized by capitalist propaganda, and declared that men and women whose lives were "so difficult and devoid of meaning while on mission to the United States" deserved some compensation for their sacrifice.

Yet his was a keen intellect, capable of brilliant maneuvering, truly a product of generations of Talmudic scholars. Equipped with barely one year of formal university study, at the U.N. he was remarkably competent in the labyrinths of international politics and economic theory, and glib in statistics—often invented on the spur of the moment, but always convincing. Later he became a professor of political science, international relations, and diplomatic history.

Like other members of the Polish diplomatic corps, Katz-Suchy made it a practice frequently and vociferously to deplore the cruel necessity for being away from Poland, where life was truly meaningful. To do otherwise was to run the risk of soon finding oneself back in Warsaw. In 1951, as he was making his ritual complaint about the hardships of his post at a diplomatic reception, he was rudely interrupted by Poland's Vice Minister of Foreign Affairs, who said: "I agree with you. Time to go home." The order was irrevocable, and the Katz-Suchy family returned to Poland soon thereafter, with enough American supplies to equip a small army. Unfortunately, by then my life had become inextricably entangled with his.

I was not yet an American citizen, and accepted a Polish passport only after considerable persuasion by my uncle. He had not told me that he was under party pressure to return all his family to Poland. Soon I received a summons from Warsaw to report to Geneva for an assignment at the Economic and Social Council of the U.N. After a grimly disillusioning month of home leave in a Poland held fast in the iron grip of the Stalinists, I was sent to the Paris sessions of the U.N. General Assembly, where the atmosphere was no less oppressive. As Stalin's growing paranoia enveloped the Polish delegation, I felt that I was at the mercy of my Polish superiors. I feared that as a result of having accepted the Polish passport I would end up against my will in Poland, separated from my husband and little boy.

I discovered that Katz-Suchy was unwilling to make the smallest effort in my behalf. In fairness, he may have been unable to do so. Once I heard him tell a group of younger members of the Paris delegation that he was the son of a Polish peasant, and had "slept on straw" in his childhood. He was not the only highly-placed Jewish Communist to attempt to rewrite his biography during this period.

After I returned to the United States, which is another story, I saw my uncle for the last time, in New York in 1952, when he came as a delegate to the U.N. General Assembly. Relations between us were strained, for I had left my job at the delegation and was about to give up my Polish passport. The Polish Communist Party had entrusted him with the job of "convincing" my husband and myself to move to Poland, for it was felt that we "knew too much." He did its bidding, applying every ounce of cunning he possessed, but he failed.

Our last encounter took place shortly after the frame-up trial of Rudolf Slansky, former secretary-general of the Czechoslovak Communist Party, in which the prosecution had been blatantly anti-Semitic. When I questioned the brutality of the death sentences hurriedly meted out to Slansky and his co-defendants, my uncle, extremely agitated, countered with slogans: "The party is always right. The death penalty is the highest defense of the proletarian state."

His career seemed to go along smoothly for a time, for he was named Poland's ambassador to India in 1953. Several years later he was demoted to a professorship at the Institute of Political Science in Warsaw. In 1968, along with other Polish Jews who were victims of Gomulka's anti-Jewish purge, he was deprived of his livelihood. Dismissed from his teaching post on charges of supporting the "Zionism" he had spurned and ridiculed all his adult life, he was allowed to go into exile in Denmark in 1969. He remained adamant to the end. In 1970 he told a *New York Times* reporter: "I'm still a Pole and Poland will always be my country . . . I still believe in socialism and that the future is socialism." A year later, at the age of 58, he suffered a fatal heart attack.

He visited Israel several times during the two years of his Danish exile. Though met with skepticism in many quarters, he reportedly was a guest of the government and was considered for a professorship at Tel Aviv University, arranged, so rumor had it, by radical friends from pre-war Poland then settled in Israel. I found it difficult to reconcile this story with the fact that my uncle had for years served one of Israel's greatest enemies and, moreover, was publicly unrepentant. In 1971, in Jerusalem, a cousin summed it up for the Israelis: "He was, after all, a Jew." Would my uncle Benzion have agreed with this assessment?

Though his style was quieter and less flamboyant, Benzion too was a deeply political man. Nor was his career, like Judah's, lacking in disappointments and paradoxes. But the central premise of his life— the return of the Jewish people to Palestine—had been achieved. He was grateful to the State of Israel, he told us on a visit to New York, for the simplest of reasons: "There I walk the streets as a free man."

At the beginning, acceptance was not easily attained. Because he, his wife, and young son arrived only in 1939, smuggled out of Poland soon after the outbreak of World War II with the help of the World Zionist Organization, they had to struggle to win the recognition of their peers. Pioneer Zionists, who had come years and even generations earlier, did not always welcome relative newcomers with open arms. While it had occurred to him, he once told us, tongue-in-cheek, simply to claim the crown on the grounds of his descent from the House of David, he knew that full membership in the community depended on proving himself. This he proceeded to do by using all the powers of his intellect and his devotion to the Zionist cause, fighting for his new homeland in the 1948 War of Independence and later participating in high councils of the state.

I rediscovered my uncle Benzion when he first came to New York, in 1953. At this juncture he was a noted Hebrew scholar and poet, and a lecturer in classical literature at Tel Aviv University. Benzion was the author of more than twenty books, the translator of Omar Khayyam and Aeschylus into Hebrew.[1] He was expert in Persian, Greek, Arabic,

---

1. Among the books written by Benzion Katz are *Metrics in Bialik's Poetry* (1943), *Hebrew Literature Between Two Wars* (1953), *Jerusalem Sonnets* (1965), and

and Latin, as well as Hebrew, and fluent in all the European and some esoteric languages. He headed the Jewish Agency's Youth and Hechalutz Department from 1941 to 1963, his chief mission being to encourage young people to settle or at least to study in Israel. He traveled a good deal, but his real ambition was to have more time for scholarly studies and writing poetry.

We met when Katz-Suchy was applying pressure from afar for me to return to Poland. Benzion's reassuring presence, his kindness and concern, did much to assuage our anxieties and to keep us resolute in our decision not to submit. He could be fascinating on a wide variety of subjects, and retained his special brand of humor as well as his family sentiment. We found him modest, and totally indifferent to material possessions.

Leading Jewish personalities flew to New York from all over the country to confer with him, and he traveled to other cities. Meetings went on all day and into the night. Yet he always found time to visit us, coming by bus and subway after long workdays. His clear appraisal of the Soviet Union and his vast store of information on its involvement in the Middle East were particularly helpful in transforming my own political views. Each time he went back to Israel we found the parting more difficult. The impact of his strong Jewish identity was enormous, resulting in my developing an abiding interest in the history and traditions of my people and an intense attachment to Israel.

During the last years of his life he achieved the honor of becoming the first rector of Tel Aviv University, as well as head of its Department of Classical Studies. He brought my mother to Israel. She became ill and, until her death, required infinite attention that made great demands on his heavy schedule.

My last memory of Benzion dates from the spring of 1967, a few months before the Six Day War. He had come to New York to alert the American Jewish community to Israel's emergency. He seemed profoundly depressed by the war that loomed threateningly on the horizon, and the lack of concern among many American Jews. Who would have believed then that the prospect of Israel's extinction would elicit such depths of commitment from American Jewry? In November 1968

Creative Paths, a collection of literary essays (1966). His translations into Hebrew include selections from the Persian epic *Shah-nameh* by Firdusi, and several classical Greek works.

he died suddenly in Israel at age sixty-two, after routine eye surgery. His loss was deeply mourned by the academic community and the nation at large. Said one Israeli newspaper: "Heads of state, the academic corps, statesmen and students accompanied . . . the Rector of Tel Aviv University on his last journey . . . . With his death ends a whole era in the history of the University and its development."

Much of his work remained unfinished; Israel needed him. His achievements have been largely ignored by major reference texts, which feature Juliusz Katz-Suchy as a prominent Jew. Perhaps this is to be expected, for public attention usually is drawn more to the notorious than to the pure of heart. I too have devoted more space to the younger than the older brother, perhaps because villainy is more interesting than goodness, and the process of transformation from decency to villainy the most fascinating of all.

Could I ever forgive my uncle Katz-Suchy? I might overlook his ruthlessness where my safety was concerned as opposed to his solicitude for himself, but he remains the assassin of my youthful dream. A selfless revolutionary became a tool of party power, and thus personified for me the bankruptcy of his ideology. Yet his death made it possible once more to mourn for the young idealist he had been.

If the tragedy of Benzion's death was that he had so much still to give, the tragedy of Katz-Suchy's was his inability to the very end to admit that he had misspent his life in a false cause that finally betrayed him.

"My Uncles Judah and Benzion" is the work of a much more mature — and thoroughly disillusioned — person. I had been to postwar Poland and seen "socialism" at work. The essay was published in the premier issue of Present Tense, in 1973, and earned rave reviews. I was told years later by the magazine's editors that it had generated the largest amount of mail in the history of the magazine. The "Judah" of this essay is, of course, the same person as "Janek" of "Son of Poland."

My Father, the Socialist

It was autumn 1951. I sat alone in a dingy, unheated room of the Polish Ministry of Foreign Affairs in Warsaw. Before me stood three brown cartons containing my father's papers. I had delivered them in New York to my uncle, Juliusz Kats-Suchy, Poland's U.N. representative, on specific request of the Polish government. I had not looked at them since 1945. In a moment I would be unraveling the past.

Two days after my father's funeral, his New York landlady had asked me to vacate his quarters. She had been very fond of him, but the housing shortage was acute. It was with considerable effort that my husband and I (we had been married just six months) accomplished our task. My father's room was strewn with papers, books, and magazines—the tools of his daily endeavors. A pen was at his desk, as if waiting to be picked up. The room seemed still warm with his presence. Only there did it seem to me that my father had gone out for just a moment and would soon be returning, and I did not want to destroy this temporary illusion. I knew, as I packed his belongings, that he would not return, not ever again. I put aside a crumpled note to me found in the pocket of his bathrobe; it was written following one of his lighter heart attacks several months earlier. "Dearest Irena," it said. "In a few moments I shall take another pill. If I should not wake up do not grieve over me too much. I have lived out my life, yours still stands before you. Be well, both of you, be happy." My father was then fifty-one years old. In a drawer was another letter containing the political credo of this man, who for several years lived with a presentiment of his own death. "My ideal has been an independent, socialist, democratic Poland, for which I have fought since 1909. I have never betrayed my socialist principles. I have believed in an understanding and friendship between Poland and the U.S.S.R. only in the interests of my own country. My attitude toward the Communist party has remained negative." This I also kept. It would not be in the boxes I was to open in the Ministry of Foreign Affairs.

Before World War II we had lived in southern Poland. My father was a successful lawyer, and my life might have been typical of other middle-class children. There were two factors, however, that seriously affected what might otherwise have been a complacent existence—my family was Jewish, and my father, a leftist socialist, insisted on being active in the political life of our country. Unlike his brothers, who had emigrated to America in their youth, he had remained tied to Poland. From the instant he joined a student revolutionary organization (Promien) concerned not only with socialism but with Poland's struggle for independence, he was to remain that country's devoted champion. The next steps were membership in the Polish Socialist Party (PPS) and the Jewish Bund.

To some men political battle is the staff of life. Without it they wilt and die. Such a man was my father. In the injustices existing in his country he found his challenge, and in their ultimate solution, his goal. To the realization of socialist principles he devoted a major portion of his energies, emotion, and intellect. Following graduation from a Polish Gymnasium he entered the University of Cracow to study law, obtaining the degree of doctor of law. World War I, to which as a follower of the French socialist Jaurès, he was deeply opposed, interrupted his studies, and he became a first lieutenant in the Austrian army. He lived through the carnage without having fired a single shot—always a source of enormous satisfaction to him.

When the war was over he returned to his half-ruined city in the newly created, independent Poland to organize a peasant and workers' council. He spoke to a crowd of thousands who had come from the surrounding hills and mountains to celebrate the beginning of a democratic republic. Shortly afterward, his hopes for a socialist Poland were dashed by Pilsudski's regime. He was sent with other socialists to a detention camp for several months. Here his most durable friendships in the Jewish Bund were formed.

Having married the daughter of a prominent Jewish family in 1921, and after completing the four years of required legal clerkship, my father opened his own law office. Despite his radical involvements and his willingness to take on unpopular political cases (often without a fee), he went on to become one of the country's top lawyers. The Cracow bar appointed him official lecturer on criminal law, which was his specialty, and he often appeared jointly with Leib Landau, Poland's greatest criminal lawyer.

As a result of my father's radical views and those of my mother's younger brother Judah, a communist, my childhood was one of continuous upheaval. There was the constant surveillance by the secret police as well as the threat and actuality of jail and concentration camp to my loved ones. One of the sharpest memories of my Polish childhood is the incessant ringing of the doorbell in winter darkness of early morning or in the hazy dawn of spring, followed by a sudden stirring of the household, quick steps in the hall. This was the so-called "rewizja," a thorough search of the contents of the house for incriminating evidence of subversion. The secret police were notorious for fabricating such evidence where none existed by planting Communist material in the homes of socialists. (The Communist Party was illegal and operated underground. The penalty for membership was a long prison term or the concentration camp.)

On occasion, following an intensive search, our visitors would produce a warrant for my father's arrest. The Polish judicial system knew no right of bail. When arrested, even political prisoners remained incarcerated until brought to trial. The case against my father was usually so flimsy that it never reached the courts, with one exception, when it was dismissed after a day's proceedings. The raids usually came just before the first of May. By arresting leaders of the Socialist Party on the eve of traditional May Day protest demonstrations, the police hoped to cripple their size and militancy and to intimidate the participants.

The first of May 1937 passed without the expected visit from the police. My father made a speech in the market square, concluding with one of the Socialist Party's most popular slogans: "Down with the concentration camp at Bereza Kartuska!" Several days later he was on a train bound for that very camp. Could the regime succeed in illegal imprisonment of Socialists? This would be a test for which three party leaders from the provinces were chosen—all of them attorneys, all Jews. The secret police came directly to my father's office and took him away.

Our front bell and the phone rang incessantly that day. Scores of people expressed anger and concern. Above my father's abandoned office desk hung a huge portrait of Karl Marx. On his last birthday, the socialist workers' orchestra from the large railroad yards had played "The Red Flag" outside our front door to surprise him. All of them then came in to pump his hand and have a thimbleful of vodka. Now he was gone to we knew not what awful fate.

My mother left at once for Warsaw to confer with leaders of the PPS. The arrest constituted a dangerous precedent, and the party privately threatened the prime minister with a general strike. After a week of negotiations this warning obtained his release. He came back looking years, not days, older. A large cake from the Jewish "kehillah" with the words "Mazel tov!" in chocolate frosting stood on the dining room table as he told us about the horrors of the concentration camp.

The constant hounding of my father and my young uncle for their courageous identification with Poland's masses awakened in me too a consciousness of the lot of those who toiled and suffered all about me: the worker who lived in a hovel, labored long hours for meager pay under constant threat of unemployment and starvation, and was shot at when he marched in protest; the often hungry peasant who went to sleep at sunset to conserve oil, and whose children, burdened by adult chores and national neglect were doomed to continue their fathers' tradition of illiteracy. I was conscious too of the lot of the ghetto-spawned Polish Jew who carried on his bent back not only the weight of his own dreadful poverty and second-class citizenship, but also the centuries-long custom of being the scapegoat for every ill that befell his country.

My parents, unlike the generation that preceded them, were not religious Jews. They knew Yiddish but were a part of Polish life. The criticism voiced by some Poles that Jews refused to become integrated into Polish society did not apply to us. I had a special love for the Polish language and literature, the study of which I intended to make the major work of my university years. I wanted to be a Polish writer. Yet none of this managed to protect me from the anti-Semitic poison that pervaded the air. Despite this my father and other Bundists rejected a Zionist solution. Their roots in Poland were deep, going back many centuries. They would not relinquish the right to be part of its future. Not aliyah but the victory of socialism would redress the wrongs perpetrated against the Jews and establish equal rights for all minorities.

By 1938 the Western policy of appeasement had already caused the loss of the Rhineland to Germany. Ethiopia and Spain had been conquered, Austria annexed. The government of Poland, smug in a nonaggression pact with Hitler, joined the pack of wolves feasting on the corpse of its neighbor Czechoslovakia, and took a small slice of Czech territory. Few outside of the Polish Socialist Party and the Jewish Bund opposed this suicidal policy of political gangsterism to which Poland itself was to fall only a short year later.

In the summer of 1939, the year of the New York World's Fair, my father took me on a promised vacation to the United States to meet my American relatives. Due to Polish currency regulations we were able to take out only funds sufficient to last us for the two months of our intended stay. At the outbreak of the war we were stranded in the United States, almost penniless. There followed years of economic struggle and difficult adjustment. Poland plunged into the long night of German occupation, which was to end with the annihilation of its vast and important Jewish community. My father, for whom this upheaval in middle age must have been shattering, invariably showed me a cheerful face and optimistically withstood my complaints and frequent unhappiness. He displayed unusual understanding in those stormy years of my youth, which were rendered doubly hard by the occurrence of war and the necessity of exile, and rarely betrayed his own problems and doubts.

Memories passed before me quickly, fading into the present. Thirteen years had elapsed since my last glimpse of Poland. In 1951, as an employee of the Polish Delegation to the U.N., I was granted a "home leave" in Warsaw. Almost simultaneously my uncle Katz-Suchy was recalled from his New York post. For the past few weeks, in shock and disbelief, I had been witnessing "socialism at work." Crowded, unheated apartments in contrast to the luxurious villas of the security police, long queues before food shops, staggering prices and desperate, unexplained shortages, thousands of political prisoners, the lies of a regimented press.

I opened the first carton. Yellowed clippings lay on top—my father's first political steps on American soil. These were from a modest Socialist daily in New York, "Robotnik Polski" (*The Polish Worker*), of which he soon became one of the editors. At this time he supported the Polish government-in-exile as the sole free representative of occupied Poland. He dueled with the reactionary Polish daily "Nowy Swiat," and was close to the Jewish Labor Committee and the *Jewish Daily Forward*.

Behind me a door opened softly. It was my uncle Katz-Suchy. For the tall, heavy man that he was, he could at times move noiselessly and with amazing quickness.

"How are you doing?" he asked. "You know, some people are very interested in these papers, especially in the material on Oskar Lange and members of his old Socialist group."

"Who's interested?" I inquired.

"Security," was his curt reply. He watched the effect on me, and added, "I had quite a time, in fact, persuading them not to question you personally about these people." Without waiting for comment he turned on his heel and left me.

The documents of which he spoke were in a fairly neat folder. Many contained the signature and handwriting of Oskar Lange. In 1941 a group of Polish Socialists, former Cracow University students of Oskar Lange's, escaped from Poland to Sweden. They claimed to represent the Polish underground. A number of them were Jewish. Through the Jewish Labor Committee in New York my father obtained funds and visas for them and their families. He looked forward to their arrival and future collaboration. With the aid of Oskar Lange, then a professor of economics at the University of Chicago, he had recently organized the American Friends of Polish Democracy, sponsored by prominent Americans. Robert MacIver of Columbia University was chairman, with my father as executive director at a nominal salary. When his Socialist party comrades arrived, a Polish Labor Group was formed, of which he was elected chairman.

He was unprepared, however, for the intrigues and backbiting that followed. He balked at being ordered about and was removed from the chairmanship of the group, and later also from the American Friends of Polish Democracy. This was accomplished through such under-handed maneuvering by his erstwhile comrades that it resulted in strong condemnation by Oskar Lange.

Why were the security police of 1951 Poland so interested in the content of these documents? These men had been violently anti-Soviet when they clashed with my father, and the material was damaging. Later, when it became clear that leftist forces were winning in Poland, the most vehemently anti-Soviet members of the Polish Labor Group began flirting with the new Polish government. One of them even returned to Poland and was the editor of a leading daily. Several others obtained well-paid positions in the U.N. Secretariat. Because they re-mained Polish subjects, the government in Warsaw could have them ousted from their jobs. Even Lange did not escape unscathed in these papers. Worried about his American citizenship, he was reluctant to involve himself publicly with the leftist group of intellectuals later organized by my father to support the Lublin government—the first government of postwar Poland. Lange was now a deputy in the Polish "Sejm" (Parliament) and a man of some influence. I thought I was contributing a slice of history to the government archives. Had I sus-pected that the security police were interested in these papers, I would never have surrendered them.

Deeply hurt by his Socialist comrades, rejected by the Polish army in Canada as too old, my father abruptly decided to end his political career and to contribute to the Allied defense as a lathe operator. In January 1943 he collapsed at his machine. By the time I was called the verdict was in—a serious heart attack. It was touch and go for the first few weeks, and my world was plunged into despair. I could not con-ceive of my father dying, and tenaciously held onto the shreds of hope that remained.

He lived. Six weeks after the attack he came out of the hospital, walking and speaking with difficulty. He spent some weeks in a convalescent home, and as soon as he was sufficiently recovered he moved into a furnished room on the upper West Side of Manhattan. (I was a student and lived in the International House.) He slowly emerged from political oblivion, and his room again filled up with newspapers and magazines.

Among émigré circles in Great Britain and the United States great influence was wielded at this time by a former minister in the Pilsudski government, Colonel Ignacy Matuszewski. With the death of Premier Sikorski in an airplane accident (he had signed a pact of understanding with the Soviet Union), the Polish government-in-exile openly took an anti-Soviet position. The émigrés of all shades of political opinion followed suit. Thus, former political prisoners in prewar Poland, liberals, Socialist and Peasant Party members, afraid lest they be called unpatriotic, fell under the spell of Matuszewski's pen. History witnessed a sudden unity between the fascist and the democratic elements among Polish émigrés, the liberals becoming apologists for Polish reaction. Following the outbreak of hostilities between Germany and the Soviet Union, paradoxically, all the force of Polish opinion was turned against the latter. One would have thought, in looking over Polish press clippings of that period, that between 1939 and 1944 Poland was actually at war with the Soviet Union, and that the conflict with Germany was an inconsequential side issue—a mere accident.

In April 1943 came the uprising in the Warsaw ghetto. For my father it was indeed a turning point. The Polish government-in-exile failed to issue orders to the Polish underground, which it controlled, to aid the Jews fighting in the ghetto's inferno. Brutal details of those terrible weeks had been made available to the Jewish Bund in New York, and I found my father profoundly shaken. Then came the protest suicide of his friend and comrade in the Bund, Szmuel Zygelbojm, in London. The Polish government remained unresponsive. Instead, General Anders, commander of the Polish army with the British in the Middle East, promised his troops that on their return to liberated Poland they would eliminate the remnants of its Jewry. This pronouncement was the single most important factor in my father's decision to wage relentless battle with the Polish government in London.

The prospect of returning to a prewar type of dictatorship and anti-Semitism was unthinkable. At the same time, the Soviet Union appeared to have relaxed its rigid control over world Communist parties and was fighting on the Allied side. Over-optimism and self-delusion? In this view they had a lot of illustrious company, including that of the President of the United States. As a direct result of this thinking my father helped to form a group of Polish liberals in opposition to the London government. This included Oskar Lange, Julian Tuwim, Poland's greatest contemporary poet, who was Jewish, and the famed artist Artur Szyk. It was a period during which my father was much maligned. Liberals joined with the most rabidly reactionary elements among the Poles in hounding and reviling him. Democratic forces refused to give him an arena for expression, and he was forced to send his writings to the Polish and American Communist press. Throughout those heartbreaking years, despite the barrage of insults and accusations, he sincerely believed that he was working for Poland's sake.

Before me lay the manuscript of a modest pamphlet, published with private donations from friends, just one year after his heart attack. It was entitled "The Future Government of Poland," and was a typical lawyer's brief, logical and precise. Some days after publication the Soviet news agency Tass cabled its contents to Moscow. Soon *Pravda* carried a news item on its first page. Two days later coverage appeared in *The New York Times,* and *Time* magazine followed. A Polish Socialist proved the illegality of the Polish government-in-exile. By its own admission it had been a continuation of the prewar Polish government. The latter, my father claimed, had been based on an illegally adopted constitution.

This constitution was created in 1935 in order to give Marshal Pilsudski a virtual dictatorship. The constitutional proposals were then rammed through the Sejm (Parliament) without the benefit of a quorum. My father's thesis, deceptively simple, was precisely what the Soviet Union and the Polish left needed to establish a legal basis for a new government in postwar Poland. The pamphlet called for the resignation of all democratic forces from the government-in-exile (causing a furor among his Socialist comrades who participated in the London government), then for the formation of a world-wide Polish Committee of National Liberation, which would eventually become the provisional government in liberated Poland. New election laws would be promulgated and free elections then held. The plan was broadcast all over the world, and my father became an important element in the politics of the Poland-to-be.

From London came private admonitions from his Socialist friends. One wrote a particularly vindictive letter, which now lay among these papers. This same man later joined the present Polish government, and watched silently over the demise of civil liberties and the Socialist party. The reaction of the Jewish Bund in New York produced the greatest pain. His comrades there accused him of being in the pay of Stalin—almost a deathblow to his Socialist pride. His courage in the face of all this vilification was remarkable, and prompts me to say that he would not have given up his convictions in the face of the later Communist takeover in Poland, as Lange and Cyrankiewicz[1] had done. Always a fighter, he would more likely have been killed, as was his close friend Jan Masaryk.[2]

I put aside a sheaf of clippings. These were his letters, published in *The New York Times*, the *Herald Tribune*, and *P.M.*, and a series of article in *New Masses*, calling for a reconciliation between the two existing Polish governments. He was a prolific letter writer, and his comments were invariably printed. With no official status, and no funds, he was the focus of all activity in Polish émigré circles. People were either enthusiastically for him or bitterly against him. He may have been described as a hero or a devil, but he was never ignored.

I was now looking at the record of a year of major happenings. A second front had been established in Europe. The Red Army was in control of a large part of Polish territory. A Committee of National Liberation was formed, as projected by my father. Mikolajczyk, the premier of the government-in-exile, made a trip to Moscow. A "rapproachment" seemed possible. But the Polish government vacillated, refusing to give in on the question of the 1935 constitution. In the meantime the Committee of National Liberation was in Poland, entrenching itself, organizing support, and restoring order. On January 5, 1945 the U.S.S.R. recognized the Lublin government as the Provisional Government of Poland. Following Yalta, this became the Provisional Government of National Unity, and included Mikolajczyk only as a vice-premier. Many Poles heretofore opposed to the new Polish government began switching their allegiance. There was a good deal of talk that my father would be named Poland's ambassador to Washington.

At this time, the official line of the Polish Communists was that there was no need to repeat the experience of the U.S.S.R. In Poland,

---

1. Leader of the postwar Socialist party.
2. Masaryk became minister of foreign affairs in postwar Czechoslovakia, and was murdered by its Communist regime.

socialism would be achieved without the violence and disruption of its Soviet predecessor. According to the party's spokesman, Wladyslaw Gomulka, there would be no necessity for a dictatorship of the proletariat. Socialism would be achieved through evolutionary means; collectivization would be dispensed with. The government included many Socialists, and for a brief spell Poland enjoyed the novelty of political freedom.

The death of Franklin Delano Roosevelt came in April 1945, on the eve of the San Francisco Conference on International Organizations, which was to lay the foundation of the United Nations. A short time earlier, the Polish Press Agency (Polpress) had opened an office in New York City. My father went to San Francisco as its correspondent. The new Polish government had not yet been recognized by the United States. In the event of recognition, he was to be its representative to the Conference.

I had not seen my father as happy as on that day in May 1945 when he left on a special train carrying hundreds of newspapermen and radio commentators to San Francisco. There he was in his element at last, busy from dawn until late at night, a familiar figure on the conference scene, constantly making friends for the new Poland.

The anticipated recognition of the Lublin government occupied the headlines of the hour. Had it come about during the Conference, my father would have been catapulted into international prominence— but history ruled otherwise. The Polish American Congress, in a desperate move to prevent recognition, asked Edward R. Stettinius, Jr., head of the U.S. delegation, to press the Soviet Union on the issue of sixteen Poles arrested on charges of diversionary activities against the Red Army. A huge press conference was called. The room was packed for the dramatic announcement. Sixteen "democratic" Poles were being held unjustly, said Stettinius. Then came a question from the representative of Polpress (my father). "Mr. Secretary, do you happen to know who they are?" Mr. Stettinius faltered. The man from Polpress then took out a list and proceeded to read names, one by one. Several of them, he said, were well-known fascists and anti-Semites. The reporters ran for the telephones.

From that moment, everything the man from Polpress said was news. His embarrassing question reverberated in conference corridors and in the press. James Reston wrote about it at length in *The New York Times,* and other newspapers and magazines covered the incident. In retrospect, I can understand why my father played this role. He still fully believed that the Lublin government was independent of the

Soviet Union, and that Soviet support was being given without conditions attached. His naivete and trust now seem astounding. I agreed with him at the time—a fact that causes me considerable anguish.

It was also in San Francisco that he met again with his old colleague and friend, Jan Masaryk, Foreign Minister of Czechoslovakia.

My uncle was by my side. Once again he had come in as stealthily and softly as a cat.

"How are you progressing?" he asked. "What's that?" He picked up a large photograph of my father with Jan Masaryk taken by a newspaper photographer in San Francisco. Masaryk had been a huge man, and he towered above my father.

"You'd better get rid of that," he advised. When I walked out of the Ministry that day, I took the photograph. It is still a constant reminder that in the "People's Democracies" there was no place for either man.

Recognition of the Lublin government by the United States and Great Britain came in July 1945. After the Potsdam Declaration of the Big Three, the Polish government-in-exile virtually ceased to exist.

In late 1945 my father was contemplating a return to Poland. He had no funds for such a journey, and none were offered by the Lublin government, to which he had been so loyal. In November of that year, Oskar Lange went to Poland. He had been summoned there to be named Poland's ambassador to the United States. When I later questioned my Communist uncle Katz-Suchy about that appointment, he said bluntly, "Your father's first name (Abraham) was so unmistakably Jewish we couldn't name him ambassador. We had to take Lange, with the complication of his American citizenship." (The Poles had never heard of Abraham Lincoln!)

In the fall of 1945 several important appointments on this continent had already been made, and my father went to Washington to confer with Polish Embassy officials and to see Mrs. Lange, newly installed at the embassy. He came back upset by the caliber of the people being appointed. He was particularly disturbed that Count Jan Drohojowski was appointed as Poland's minister to Mexico. How could a member of the Polish nobility represent a government of workers and peasants? It was the first dent in his confidence in the Lublin government.

Oskar Lange landed at LaGuardia Airport early in December. A group of Poles, my father among them, was there to meet him. Later my father took him aside and asked, "Did you bring news for me, Oskar?" "No," was the cold reply.

That night we visited my father, and it saddened me to see his sudden discouragement and obvious depression. He was sitting before his old typewriter, on which he had typed so many thoughtful letters and so many appeals, using the two-finger method. He was slowly pecking again, but the usual enthusiasm had gone out of him.

Several days later he suffered an attack of appendicitis. The operation was hazardous because the physician had delayed too long, worrying about his heart condition. The patient looked surprisingly well after the surgery. When I was leaving he asked, "Was there any mail for me from Washington?" There had been no mail. Several days earlier, Boleslaw Gebert, formerly a CIO official and head of the Polish section of the International Workers Order, a good friend, had called him and said, "I'm not supposed to tell you, but there is a great and wonderful surprise in store for you." Later, Gebert bitterly reproached himself for not having said more.

The following morning I called the doctor.

"Your father's condition has worsened," I was told.

"How much?"

"I don't have much hope. It's his heart."

At the hospital, where he was a ward patient, we were told that he had not yet been put on the critical list; therefore permission to see him outside visiting hours would have to be granted by the chief surgeon. The surgeon was in the operating room. My husband and I sat in the hospital lobby all that Saturday afternoon waiting for him to finish the operation. I bitterly regretted our lack of money, which had made it necessary for my father to be placed in the ward.

At six o'clock the surgeon finally pronounced my father's condition critical. When we entered his room we were immediately struck by the sight of the oxygen tent under which he lay. He had a terrible hacking cough, which became more and more frequent as night came on. He had been doing a lot of thinking about Poland.

"I thought of a wonderful plan," he said. Much later, when his breathing became more labored and purple circles formed under his eyes, he said, "It was a rather stupid idea I had, anyway."

Several times he urged me to go home because I would be tired the next day. At three a.m. he suddenly began to choke. A nurse went for the intern on duty. His head slumped, his eyes closed. I could not bear it, and I ran out of the room. My husband came after me. I stood in the hallway and uttered aloud the awful words, "He's dead, isn't he?"

The intern was giving him a last, useless interjection. The next thing I heard was the sound of the oxygen tent being taken down. It was all over. I could not look at my father dead. We walked down the stairs. There were papers to be signed. The intern said, "The nicest people always die." We walked out into the cold night, leaving behind us the body of my father, our dearest friend, a Pole, a Jew, a Socialist, and a kind and good man.

Early in the morning, arrangements were made for the funeral. Members of my father's group were deeply shocked. Moments after they were called, they were back on the phone.

"Ambassador Lange has just come into town especially to see Dr. Penzik and to bring him personally the news of a tremendously important appointment."

"Tell him he's just a little late," I said.

The funeral home was packed with high officials of the new Polish government, including Ambassador Lange, the Poles with whom he had worked, relatives, friends, comrades from the Jewish Bund, and former inhabitants of our Polish town. A rabbi chanted Hebrew prayers over the body of my father,s an atheist. I sat in the back listening to the Poles' eulogies, which were now meaningless.

He died as a charity patient, without the constant attendance of a doctor, not knowing that his efforts on Poland's behalf had been noted by the government. A day later, after his appointment, he would have been under the finest of care. Specialists would have been bending over him to try to ease his pain. Perhaps he could have been saved. Perhaps the knowledge that he was remembered might have given him the strength to survive.

At the cemetery, flowers and Polish banners stood all around us in total disregard of its Orthodox policies. A member of the Jewish Bund spoke over his grave. "Shalom, chaver Penzik," he said. "Peace be with you, comrade Penzik."

In the carton lay a thin sheet of paper—a letter from the famed poet, Julian Tuwim. In the moment of my greatest despair after death, it gave me a measure of comfort.

"My dear," it said. "I am too deeply moved by the death of your unforgettable father, I respect your grief and mourning too much to write you either a simple letter of 'condolence' or to attempt to console you in your pain and loneliness. . . . You know only too well how close we were to each other, what personal and ideological friendship bound us together. . . . I knew few men with so clear a record and conscience, so passionately devoted to working for their ideals, so perpetually active. In Poland, we shall sorely miss citizen Abraham Penzik! That for which he fought and to which he devoted his strength and his health is already becoming a reality in his homeland which he loved so well. . . . And that new Poland will utter the name of Abraham Penzik with reverence. And now, dry your tears, and smile, thinking of your father, smile at those new, better times to which he gave his quiet, modest, and beautiful life." Another good man with great illusions.

Beneath the letter was the manuscript of a 1944 pamphlet entitled "Anti-Semites and Necrophiles—Remarks on the Jewish Question in Poland."

In it he analyzed the attitude of Poles toward Polish Jews between 1918 and 1939 and described the feelings of Poles during the German occupation, quoting underground newspapers in Poland. In reply to those Poles who collaborated with the Germans in the wholesale extermination of the Jewish people, one paper said: "We'll take care of our own Jews." Another stated: "The Jews are and will always be against us. . . . We have not engaged the Jews in armed battle (in prewar Poland) but now the Germans are liquidating them better and more effectively than anyone could." He spoke of the crocodile tears shed for the departed Polish Jewry by Polish officialdom in London. I read his closing words:

"Millions of Jews have already died a tragic death. Tens of thousands perished fighting for 'our freedom and yours.' But neither Polish refugees nor old Polish émigrés in the United States have managed a single action or pronouncement in this matter."

His optimism then reasserted itself:

". . . The independent Poland of the future shall be governed by the people, by peasants, workers, and the enlightened working intellectuals who constitute the majority of Poland. In the democratic people's Poland there shall be no room for national and religious struggle, for racial hatred, for any manifestation of fascism, and, therefore, for anti-Semitism."

Where was the ideal of a democratic Poland described in this pamphlet? Where were all of my father's hopes? Not in this cold, disordered room, nor in this ugly and sad building, guarded by armed militiamen. Certainly not in this city of deprivation and fear.

Searching for those ideals and hopes, I saw about me hatred, hunger, disillusion, and despair, and I knew with pain and indignation that this was not the Poland of my father's dreams. I had looked for my father's Socialist vision all of these weeks in vain—to find at last that it existed only among the pages of his old manuscripts.

These are some recollections about my father that did not belong in the Present Tense piece. I ran into quarrels among the editors of some so-called socialist magazines, and this was never published. (I withdrew it.)

Ashes to the Taste

The prisoner (my father), accompanied by two policemen, reached the small town of Bereza Kartuska in the early evening. There was a tavern on the outskirts of the town, where they stopped for a meal. The gray-haired woman behind the counter had quickly grasped the situation. "You're going to the camp, aren't you?" she asked him in hushed tones.

"Yes," he replied.

"You'd better eat well before you go, you poor soul," she said.

She turned away from him to prepare something to eat. When she looked at him again, he was surprised to see that tears had filled her eyes.

A taxi took them out of town, into the deep woods.

He saw before him, in the falling dusk, a high fence covered with barbed wire which, as he later learned, was highly electrified. A uniformed, well-armed guard let them in at the gate. The prisoner's eyes immediately fell on a row of three-story gray stone houses, former czarist army barracks. A terrible silence lay over the whole place. Another guard found his way to their side in the quickly falling darkness. The prisoner put down the small suitcase he was carrying and submitted himself to a careful scrutiny by the rough-looking, broad-shouldered man.

"A suitcase, eh? So you think you've come here for a vacation! Well, we'll give you a vacation all right," he said, and kicked over the brown leather suitcase. It fell apart.

They went to the main office in one of the buildings where the policemen, having delivered the prisoner, were dismissed, and the prisoner himself was sent to the office of the supreme commandant of the camp.

The commandant was a man of greater intelligence and refinement than any of the camp guards. His attitude was that of someone who did not like to do his job but had to, and he tried to give the impression that he was not responsible for the brutality of his subordinates.

From the office of the supreme commandant the prisoner was taken to the commandant of his particular barracks. This commandant, whose hand rested heavily on the whip lying on his desk, made no pretense. A gun was at his belt.

"Strip, you," he said. "At once!" And while the prisoner was taking off the last of what was left of his dignity, the commandant said in quick, sharp tones: "We have three rules here. One: Twenty-five lashes for the slightest disobedience. Two: Call each policeman or guard 'commandant' and follow his every order. Three: Complete silence. No one is allowed to talk. Understand?"

After the prisoner was permitted to dress, another policeman took him from the office to his barracks. The stone corridors were brightly lit and very narrow. There were doors on each side, each with a little hole in the middle. There must have been people behind those doors, but the silence was leaden and the barracks seemed dead with a heavy, terrible stillness.

The policeman opened one of the cells and pushed him in. He fell on the stone floor. His eyes slowly became used to the darkness, dimly relieved by a small oil lamp in the corner. On the floor lay eight or nine bundles of what seemed to be human bodies, in their clothing. None of them moved or said a word. The windows were closed tight and the stench that prevailed in the cell was unbearable. Weariness finally overcame him and he fell asleep.

Someone was trying to wake him up and help him get up from the floor. Startled out of his sleep, he picked up his weary bones with an effort and stood in line with the other prisoners. His watch told him it was four in the morning. The door had opened swiftly and in came a stocky policeman, heavily armed. The men stood at attention. The tormentor counted them off, remarking: "A new one, eh?" Then they marched off, probably to breakfast. "You stay here, new one, you'll get nothing to eat today."

"To the wall, march! Turn around! Turn around, I said!" The whip whistled in the silence of the room. "Bend your knees, lower! You Socialist son of a ——! Hands up! Now remain in this position until I give the order!"

Two hours later he was still in the same position. Blood had drained from his hands, which became white and lifeless and were slowly coming down in spite of his efforts to hold them up. His knees trembled. Once, his tormentor walked out, and a few other prisoners returned. He could not see the door, and he remembered the commandant's first rule—twenty-five lashes for the slightest disobedience. Then someone whispered: "Hold on!"

One hour later, as he was about to faint, the policeman became bored with his play.

"Get up and strip!" he growled. His hands did not want to obey him. The whip came closer and closer. It had awakened his hands, and he began to undress feverishly. Then with his clothes in his hands, with the policeman at his heels, he was rushed by the sound of the whip, nude and breathing heavily, through the narrow corridors, up the stairs to the attic. The trip upstairs was accompanied by frequent commands: "Lie down! Get up! Get up, you! Lie down! Bend your knees! Get up!" In the attic ne put his bundle of things next to all the others. He was then permitted to put on his jacket and pants.

The camp barber was the next stop. His hair was completely shaved off and, under orders, he stooped down and picked up each and every hair from the floor and took it to the latrine, accompanied by his ever-present guard.

The latrine presented a terrible sight. The prisoners were taken there but once a day, and were given about one minute's time. Where there was room for three, twenty-five or thirty would go in at the same time. "Hmm! Looks like this place needs a cleaning," was the comment from behind. "Prisoner 1177 [by this time he had acquired a number], bend down and start cleaning! Yes, with your hands, if you don't mind! What is it? Not good enough for you? Well, maybe this will be!" The whip whistled again. The odor in the place was horrible. The prisoner, the great lawyer, looked at his hands. They were strong and handsome. Hands that had held a pen, maybe a rifle in the last war, mostly books, sometimes people's lives. A new job for his hands might do them a world of good.

He bent down and began his task.

At the end of the week a delegation from the Minister of the Interior arrived on its monthly visit. Its job was to talk to prisoners and offer them declarations to sign that were to speed up their release. To sign them was to agree to end all political activity. A few signed; the majority never did.

"Do you know why you are here?" asked the Minister's delegate, with a wry smile. Prisoner 1177, a little bent, somewhat aged, and wearing dirty, wrinkled clothes, answered calmly: "Yes. I am here because the administration wanted to get rid of me and could not find a legitimate way to do so."

What insolence! But the delegate did not change his expression. The man before him was too important to be trifled with. He represented a party of great popularity and support among the workers and peasants of the country, a party as yet untouched by such drastic measures as the concentration camp. Sending him here had been an experiment, and they were awaiting the party's reaction. "I see this is quite useless. You may go," said the delegate, and he did not even offer him the declaration for a signature.

He was not surprised when a camp policeman came for him the next day, told him to gather his things, and took him out of the camp to the railroad station. "You're free," he said. "Prime Minister's orders."

These few pages were taken from my book Ashes to the Taste, *published in 1961. They illuminate my father's struggle as a socialist leader in pre-World War II Poland, ruled by the colonels, and the conditions existing in the Polish concentration camp Bereza Kartuska, created for the suppression of the communist opposition. My father's imprisonment in 1938 was a trial balloon to see if members of the PPS (The Polish Socialist Party) could be incarcerated there as well, and it failed. The Socialist Party declared a general strike. My father came home after a week. In a Warsaw photographer's studio he and another jailed socialist attorney had a memorable photograph made to show how they looked following a week in that camp. It now rests in my photo album.*

Sometime later one of the policemen who had taken my father to the concentration camp asked him to represent him in a legal dispute. He wanted to have the best possible lawyer! In New York in the 1940s, somehow a shirt from that camp numbered 1177 had arrived in my father's luggage. His Chinese laundryman then marked all his shirts with that number for identification. What irony! Until his premature death, all of my father's shirts were stamped with number 1177 in indelible ink.

On Being a Jew

Several years ago, I heard a lecture by Michael Medved at a local Orthodox synagogue. Michael had recently had a good deal of success with a book of interviews with his old high school classmates—a collaboration with David Wallechinsky—titled *Whatever Happened to the Class of '65?* The book had been purchased for television for a hefty sum and was running as a series of seamy episodes, for which Michael apologized to his audience. Its author, a recent "convert" to Orthodoxy, was now stamped with the seal of best-sellerdom and was touted as an eloquent spokesman for Judaism.

I listened with skepticism as he expounded on his strong conviction that religious beliefs coupled with temple affiliation were inseparable from Jewish identity. When I challenged him, I was described by the speaker as nothing more than a follower of the "ethical culture movement."

I cite this simplistic and uninformed judgment only because, all to often, non-believing, agnostic, or atheist Jews are made to feel that their Jewishness, indeed their very loyalty and identification with the Jewish people, are highly questionable. Frequently this is done by the zealous and dogmatic "new-born" Orthodox, whose number seems to be growing at an alarming rate, for in their estimation, they alone hold the absolute answers to the ultimate preservation of Judaic values. This attitude often does irreparable harm, alienating large numbers of interesting and caring Jews from the Jewish community.

Michael Medved notwithstanding, I was born into a prominent Jewish family in Poland and was an already conscious and identified Jewish child in the 1930s.

Like other Jewish households, ours mirrored the political ferment that had jolted Jewish society from its intellectual isolation in the ghettos. No sooner had Jews emerged from the strictures of a religious past to face the modern dilemmas of the twentieth century, than they plunged into the avant-garde of all its great socio-political movements. Our family represented three of them. Socialism was personified by my father, a labor and criminal lawyer and a prominent figure in the Polish Socialist Party. Zionism was the credo of my uncle Benzion, Communism that of my uncle Judah.

In contrast, my great-grandfather Judah Katz had been a rabbi of considerable renown, whose family had lived in Poland since the fif-

teenth century, and had at least a partly Sephardic origin. His son
Sholom, my grandfather, was also an Orthodox Jew.

On Saturdays my mother and I always went to my grandfather's for
the midday meal, which was cooked the day before and kept warm in
strict observance of the Sabbath. I came to these dinners late, straight
from school, where a six-day week prevailed. Emulating my father, I
was a militant atheist even at that early age, and week in, week out,
carrying my schoolbooks, I desecrated my grandfather's Sabbath. In
all those years of Saturdays he never indicated by word or gesture that
my disrespect for his beliefs caused him pain. Nor was there ever a
word of reproach to his son-in-law, my father, or to his son Judah for
their renunciation of religious tradition or for their political affiliations. My grandfather's tolerance was especially remarkable, because
his view of the world was that the synagogue and the Law were the
essence of life. Seen from that perspective, I can appreciate all the more
the generosity of his silence.

It was my father, more than anyone, who lent meaning and content
to my childhood. A Socialist and an atheist, he remained tied to Poland
and its political fortunes and misfortunes from his early youth. A
leading figure in both the Polish Socialist Party and the Jewish Bund—
a Jewish Socialist party that addressed itself primarily to the needs of
the Jewish proletariat—he was a leader, an intellectual with a daring
mind, always bursting with new concepts and ideas. Above his desk
hung a portrait of Karl Marx, and on his desk stood a photograph of
Vladimir Medem, a leader of the Jewish Bund—his two loyalties.
Along with tomes by Marx and Engels, he read all the contemporary
Yiddish writers, subscribed to the Yiddish press, spoke an impeccable,
literary Yiddish, and identified fully with the needs of the Jewish
working class.

The Poland in which we lived was riddled with anti-Semitism, and
my father suffered because of his secular Jewish commitment and his
Socialist ideology. On occasion he spent sojourns as a political prisoner
in a Polish jail, and once, a week in Poland's only concentration camp.

Marshal Pilsudski's one-party government tolerated the existence
of a large Jewish minority (3.5 million in a population of nearly 35
million), provided they were "good" Jews, loyal to the Marshal. But
my father was an implacable opponent. After the Marshal's death, in
1935, the ruling colonels openly sanctioned anti-Semitic outrages by
the Nationalist party. In 1936, Prime Minister Skladkowski officially
approved all the excesses with this statement: "My government considers that no one in Poland should be injured. An honest host does not

allow anyone to be harmed in his house. But an economic fight, why not?" Six hundred years after King Casimir the Great had guaranteed Jewish settlement in Poland, we Jews were not only second-class citizens but "guests" in our own country.

Because they believed that there was no future for Jews in Poland, Zionists such as my uncle Benzion thought tat Jewish energies had to be applied exclusively to the cause of a Jewish homeland. The Socialists, including the Jewish Bund, categorically rejected the Zionist solution. Since the colonels were eager to rid Poland of Jews, the Socialists went so far as to hurl charges of "collaboration" at the Zionists. My father and my uncle Judah, for whom the Polish government was the ultimate foe, thought that Zionism, with its counsel of eventual departure, would play directly into the enemy's hands. They supported the socialist credo that Jews must stay in Poland and fight for a better life for all, and that, along with Poland's other economic and social problems, injustice against Jews would be eliminated only through the victory of socialism.

Of the three ideologies represented by my family I was most attracted to my father's. I was not a guest in my country, despite the prime minister's pronouncement. My roots were deep, going back many centuries, and my identification with Poland's culture and history were just as great as any Pole's—a sentiment with which many American Jews can identify.

I recall the first moment in my life that I felt myself an outcast who could never quite belong in the Poland that was my home. When I was about five my parents took me to a famous spa. In the hotel where we stayed there were no other children. Finally a little boy my age arrived, accompanied by his parents. I was overjoyed. We were inseparable for a couple of days until he asked me: "Are you Jewish? Because if you are, my parents said I cannot play with you." And I replied indignantly: "No, I'm not!" Immediately overcome by the force of that lie, I nonetheless refused to have anything more to do with him.

There were many difficult moments in my life afterward. I clearly recall wishing that I were a French, an English, or an American Jew, though never again did I consider being anything but a Jew. When I was still in grade school I had many gentile friends. The priest singled them out for their Jewish associations during a catechism class, and our relationships ceased entirely.

My family's political involvement led to a special awareness of the ominous rise of the Nazi monster across our western frontier, and to my early hatred of its ideology of brutality and murder. In the summer of 1939, my father took me on a promised vacation to see the New York World's Fair. World War II broke out three days before we were scheduled to sail back to Europe. My father connected with the Jewish Bund in New York, and became active among Jewish émigrés and Polish-Americans—to whom he was a double anathema, as a Socialist and a Jew. Eventually I went to Columbia University on a scholarship.

For Polish Jews, 1939 was the beginning of a horrible nightmare that ended in almost total annihilation. Herded into ghettos and ultimately into cattle cars, they fulfilled Hitler's projection of a final solution. We, in exile, were the lucky ones—we became the relics of a dying people.

There was one uplifting moment, at least for me, in those awful years—the Revolt of the Warsaw Ghetto, the brief triumph of courage over bestiality. While the Polish government-in-exile failed to give the signal for the Home Army to intervene, Szmul Zygielbojm, a Bundist leader in London, and a dear friend of my father's, committed suicide to alert the world to the imminent destruction of Polish Jewry. But his suicide was in vain; the world ignored his warning.

My father died suddenly and tragically in 1945, and it was not until a number of years later that I went back to Poland, to see "socialism at work." I returned to America convinced that my father's dream of justice, equality, decency, and the elimination of anti-Semitism under a leftist regime had been a mere illusion.

In 1953 I rediscovered my uncle Benzion, who had been smuggled into Palestine from Poland in 1939. He had become a noted Hebrew scholar and poet, the translator of Omar Khayyam and Aeschylus into Hebrew, and the head of the Jewish Agency's Youth and Hechalutz Department. In a few years he would be the first rector of Tel Aviv University. The impact of his strong Israeli identity was enormous, resulting in my developing an abiding interest in the history and traditions of my people and an identification with Israel. This last has been sorely tested in recent years by Israel's poor record with respect to the rescue of the Falashas, by its abandonment of its early Zionist ideals, by a growing militarism that goes far beyond the needs of self-defense, and, most of all, by the emergence of such personalities as Ariel Sharon. My expectations of my fellow Jews in Israel and in the Diaspora are extremely high. Too often I find them wanting. I feel a collective responsibility for the misdeeds of Jews anywhere. To me, being a Jew is equated with living a moral life of social responsibility and dedication to the highest ideals.

I never considered any other career than writing, even when I was a child. I was taught by my father's example that one had to justify one's existence by making a contribution—a difference in the world. Surrounded by social injustice and blatant discrimination against the ancient Jewish community in Poland, I became hypersensitive to all inequities.

My childhood indignation and compassion for the oppressed translated itself into a desire to change the world for the better through the use of my pen. This was also coupled with a need for immortality—everyone wants to leave footsteps in the sands of time. A very old Mordecai Kaplan told a friend of mine in Jerusalem in 1975: "Write, and you will be remembered."

Since my Jewish identity can be categorized as that of the historically conscious Jew who identifies with the history and fate of the Jewish people, I am always attracted to historical Jewish themes. I have, in fact, set myself the task of illuminating certain facets of Jewish secular history (The Bible has been covered sufficiently by others), whether they be the Bar Kochba Rebellion, the Warsaw Ghetto Revolt, the failure of Socialist Jewish leadership in Communist Poland, or the odyssey of the Western Jewish pioneer.

A writer conveys who she or he is, and I believe that the best aspects of my Jewish upbringing have taught me to seek the two essentials that must be the goal of every serious writer—truth and compassion.

Rooted in the Jewish tradition is the idea of free will: Mankind may alter its fate, or at least grapple with it. I was reared in the ideals of secular modern Jewish thinking, and I reject the old Diaspora tradition of accommodation and martyrdom for God. Instead I am always attracted to ways to combat Jewish powerlessness and themes that express it. As Mordecai Anielewicz told Emanuel Ringelblum in the Warsaw Ghetto: "The idea was to choose how to die, either like sheep for slaughter or like people of honor." A throwback to the Maccabees, to Masada, and to Bar Kochba.

Martin Buber has said: "Every moment must have in it a drop of Messianic passion." My own Jewish passion is expressed in the kind of writing I have chosen to devote my life to—in which heroic and tragic themes of Jewish history predominate. Though my profession is riddled with pitfalls, disappointments, and defeats, I persist in it because I am a Jew.

I keep a quote from the Danish philosopher Kierkegaard directly above my writing table: "There are two voices, and the first says:

'Write!' And the second voice says: 'For whom?' And the first voice answers: 'For the dead whom thou didst love.'"

So for my father, a Jew who devoted his life to a quest for justice for all mankind, for my Orthodox grandfather who had a very clear idea of why he was a Jew and still gave me the gift of his tolerance, for all those who perished in the Holocaust, for those who died for their beliefs in the Inquisition's autos-da-fé, and, yes, also for those Jews whose pioneering spirit brought them on an arduous journey to tame the Wild West, I remain a writer and a Jew.

I realize that there is some repetition here of what I wrote in "My Uncles Judah and Benzion," but a patient reader will find a good deal of my credo as a writer and a Jew in this piece. It was published in a Berkeley magazine in 1984 in response to the editor's query to various writers (including Marge Percy and Meredith Tax) about their Jewish identity.

Unfortunately, the dead "whom I didst love" were joined much later by my husband. For him too I remain a writer and a Jew.

Truth and Fiction

The Invisible Passage

This land is free, but I cannot sleep. The thunder and lightning that have passed through my life have left behind a devastated abyss. In the midst of a great city, the clanking noise of cars, trolleys, and voices of people, I hear another sound—and I cannot sleep. The hollow sound of boots is with me all night through, again and again I hear them—the sound of enslavement, the symphony of death. With a stifled cry I rise from my bed and call for Michael to comfort and protect me.

Then I remember that Michael is dead.

Michael is dead, my people are dead, and I do not deserve to live.

"If you come out of this alive, my love," he said, "take a message to the world, paint it on every neon sign in each country on this earth, avenge our death!"

The people here have been kind to me. I can live in spite of my name. I can walk in the street without a yellow armband, and I do not have to die in a ghetto. But, Michael, I cannot sleep. They come for me every night, Chaim and Anna, and little Janek, and Doctor Czerniakow and so many others, their faces livid and cold and once more I'm in the Warsaw ghetto, behind that closed wall . . . .

And then, Michael, I hear the sound of boots as on that day in April 1943 . . . .

For two years we have been living in hell. We have forgotten the meaning of the word "freedom," for the walls here are high and the gates are locked. We are jammed into overcrowded houses, compelled to live on starvation diets, deprived of medical aid and of the most elementary hygienic conveniences. We have no fuel in the extreme cold of winter, and we suffer thirst in the hot summer. We have no gas, no electricity. We are hungry, ragged, and unwashed; we have been plunged into an abyss of disease. Five hundred of us die each day. The dead are buried in mass graves. Corpses lie in the streets, covered by rags and paper. All food reserves are gone. We have even eaten the horses, and the carts carrying the dead to the cemetery are drawn by men.

You see, we are not people. We are Jews.

Often I think that no one on this earth could survive in this horror, and yet we manage to live and even to hope. I have watched so many die that I feel the burden of my twenty years a hundred times that number, lying heavily on my shoulders, for I have lived more than one lifetime of sorrow and despair.

My people are dying all around me, quietly, passively, and yet—my people desire so to live. I see that hope and terrible want in their eyes, and I turn away. Then I look for Michael, for I know that we all must die, and he knows it too. I take his hand and watch the fire in his dark eyes, and once more regain the hope that we shall die fighting on our feet, though with our backs to the ghetto wall, because Michael believes in it too.

When father was shot, many of us believed we could still be saved. When mother died of typhus, some of us still believed it. But when my little brother Janek died because he did not have enough to eat, I knew we would not survive.

Old Chaim and Anna had known me since I was born. Chaim used to bounce me on his knee and tell me terrifying stories of the powers of the "beyond" and the "unknown." Since we had all found ourselves living a terrible tale, his sad eyes rested on me often. Chaim had known about my father before we did. He had watched my mother die, and almost could not take it, for she had always been his best friend's favorite child. Chaim carried Janek to the grave, and afterwards he said:

"My child, when I see you lying there on that iron bed in the kitchen, I wonder how long we shall be able to keep you with us."

Anna shook her head and said:

"Do not talk this way, Chaim. How could God let so beautiful a girl die so young? He has left her to us to take care of, and we should be thankful that we can have her with us in this hour of trial."

But it is I am who am thankful for their love and their faithful company. We are living in a three-story, hunchbacked old house on Mila Street. It is a dreadful old house with a narrow filthy street outside. We hardly ever see the sun.

But I can live in this house of horrors and walk the dark, wet stairway to the top floor each day, because Michael lives in it too. He came to stay with us one day, quietly, after both of his parents were shot.

Michael is my tower of strength, and it is because of him that I can live. He is tall, dark, and full of an indescribable burning energy. I said that there was fire in his eyes. There is more than that. Behind that fire burns a faith so profound that it envelopes and carries away all those around him; there is nobility of soul behind that fire, and there is a warm and saddened heart.

Sometimes when I look at Michael I remember the yesterday that now seems so far off. The walks we took in the park where King Stanislaus had built his exquisite palace, the squirrels we fed, the swans on the lake, the voices of other students around us, the sky that was blue, our future that, despite anti-Semitic rumbling in our land, still seemed bright and promising. I see Michael waiting for me on the grass in front of Chopin's monument, smiling, with a load of books under his arm. Hand in hand, we walk into the sunlit street.

I remember so many things when I look at Michael.

He smiles rarely now and has no need to carry a load of books. Life has given him a diploma of maturity far more complicated than any college could have done.

Had not his professors predicted that he would make a great engineer? To prove it now he must build an invisible passage through which all of us can escape to freedom or immortality. Michael will build us that passage. I now he will.

They have left us alone for awhile, but I know they'll be back. Each night I listen for the sound of their boots, the sharp noise of bullets, the horrible cry of the tortured. They come through the gate, which is open to them but locked to us. They round up whole blocks, shoot the sick and unemployable, take the still comparatively strong to slave labor in German war industry. We Jews must make weapons to kill those who might come to save us. We Jews have no earthly right to feel or suffer like men.

We have not forgotten the months that have passed. There were 400,000 of us a year ago; there are 40,000 of us now. How could we forget?

In spite of hunger and persecution our life in the ghetto had been well organized. Behind the locked walls we had regained our spiritual and political equilibrium. A city council was set up. The connection with the Polish underground movement was established. And the Germans organized the Jewish police.

Henryk was a member of the Jewish police force. There were almost a thousand of them. They were of us, some felt as we did, and yet they were to keep us subdued. At the point of a German gun they walked through the narrow, grim streets of the ghetto and saw that we obeyed orders.

Many of them were shot, for they helped smuggle in extra food and illegal literature from the Polish underground through one of the gates. Some became creatures of the Germans. But still we received the news. When once a week long peasant carts bringing starvation rations into the ghetto began to roll over the pavements, we knew that at least one of the peasants was bringing in something much different than bread.

Henryk was a dear old friend, but we never talked about the old days. He was a few years my senior, blond, tall, and brilliant. His pleasant round face had once held many smiles. But now he had looked in the eyes of disease often, and had to turn away, for even he could not save the thousands of our children without medical supplies. Henryk, you see, was going to be a famous doctor, but Henryk became a policeman in the Jewish ghetto instead.

"I often wish I had the courage to die," he would say to me. "Yet I don't want to, not just yet. Life is too precious a thing to throw away. And I so want to see this nightmare through."

When he came to see us some nights, tired after a day of witnessing tragedy, he would talk to us about his dream for the future.

"There will be a great hospital some day on Mila Street. Children will not have to die on the sidewalks. We will give them the best of care and save them before it is too late."

Yes, we agreed, there will be a hospital . . . Henryk is a dreamer, I thought, Henryk does not know the truth.

And there was Dr. Czerniakow, chairman of the City Council and an old friend of father's, whom I frequently visited.

"You have found yourself in the midst of the greatest of crimes, my child," he would say. "We are being slowly, ruthlessly annihilated. I'm an old man, you are so young, it is a shame for you to be here. And Michael so promising, so brave, the world should belong to you both, and to many others like you, my child. But we have the misfortune of being Polish Jews. . . . We are the doomed and the unwanted. Try to live through this, child, try to see another world in which we can live and die like human beings."

"But Dr. Czerniakow, I do not believe in such a world any longer."

"You must, my child, you must. That is our only hope and salvation."

"Dr. Czerniakow, why should we wait for the world to change and let others perish all around us? If we must die, why can't we fight for our privilege to die with dignity?"

"You are so young. An uprising is a noble thing. But an uprising will mean that countless lives which might be spared will have to be laid down on the altar of sacrifice. And remember, collective responsibility is the enemy's answer to our weak attempts to resist."

"Then we must be patient and wait? For what? The Allies? The world that will hear our cry?"

"Yes, my child, we must wait."

With tears in my eyes I ran to Michael, for I knew that his answer would always be: "Fight!"

The elders did not understand. Just as in the Holy City surrounded by the Roman Legions under the leadership of Titus, the young and the old struggled in an eternal conflict. The old ones said: "Survival at any price, even at the cost of maximum compromise with the demands of the persecutor"—the young ones had replied: "We must fight!"

"Michael, we young have so much more to lose, yet we desire to fight. Why do they stop us with empty words of hope and collective responsibility?"

Michael took me by the shoulders and said:

"Do not waste your tears, my love. I promise you we shall fight. Our Jewish flag will rise high above the ghetto walls. I promise you that."

But we had no arms and we were physically exhausted. The hangman did not rest. At the end of July 1942 the Gestapo demanded from the Jewish Council that it supply for deportation to the East from 6,000 to 10,000 persons daily. Those subject to deportation were to be delivered by the Jewish police of the ghetto no later than 4 p.m. each day.

Himmler had issued an order to liquidate the ghetto. Posters appeared on the walls. They announced that 6,000 men and women were to be taken daily from the ghetto for "resettlement" purposes in the Eastern regions.

Few believed the "resettlement" tale. We had already heard of the lime-sprinkled, tightly packed railroad cars that had taken so many of us to the camp at Treblinka. Treblinka contained gas chambers, steam pipes, and the sand pits where Jews were forced to dig their own mass graves before they died.

To Dr. Czerniakow fell the honor of making the initial list of men and women to be "resettled."

We waited and held our breaths. We did not have to wait very long. At daybreak the news spread rapidly from house to house. Pale shadows wandered in the streets of the ghetto, bringing mouth to mouth information.

Dr. Czerniakow had poisoned himself.

Michael's friend, Daniel, managed to come to tell us the news despite the curfew.

"I believe Dr. Czerniakow's suicide was meant to alarm the world about the Nazi aim of our liquidation," he said.

But to us who knew him so well, the doctor's suicide had meant something more. It meant the tragic collapse of his belief in the effectiveness of the method which aimed to avert a clash with the enemy, to execute their orders, and try to survive at any price. Dr. Czerniakow saw that there was no price that would leave even the smallest chance for the Jews of the ghetto to live, and so he chose to die.

"I think Dr. Czerniakow's duty was to call the population to active resistance against the invader, instead of this hopeless gesture," Daniel's voice sounded hollow and bitter.

"He's done his best, Daniel, in the light of his convictions. The call to arms, that is our duty!" Michael replied.

Many reported voluntarily at the deportation center on Stawki Street. I stood in front of our house and watched them go by though tears blinded my eyes. They left in thousands, carrying their little bags of clothing with them, their faces expressionless, empty—like a herd of cattle patiently and slowly going to their death. Little children tagged along at their mothers' skirts, and bearded old men walked among them with quiet dignity. There was fear in the eyes of some, despair in some, and even hope in others.

They were going to embrace freedom outside the ghetto wall—eternal freedom, I guess.

Henryk and others like himself were responsible for their arrival on Stawki Street. That first night Henryk came in to see us. His young face was ashen gray and deeply lined.

"They pack them in in hundreds where there's room for tens, they seal the carts, and send them to their destination! Our people are slowly dying a horrible death in those cars! Is there no hope left?"

I had never seen Henryk cry before. But he sat down on our crooked kitchen stool, buried his head in his hands, and wept like a child. We let him battle with his grief alone, Michael and I.

That night Michael spoke at a secret meeting in one of the large cellars, and called openly for organized action.

"Jews, citizens, brothers in slavery! All of us here realize that 'resettlement' is a myth, a brutal and clever lie thrown brazenly into our faces by the Nazis. We can choose to believe it and die a patient death of martyrs or we can face the truth presented by the testimony of the members of our police force and several persons who have escaped from the trains. The time for action is *now*. We must put a stop to this mass murder by refusing to die like cattle. The question is set before you clearly. Are you prepared to face it?"

The elders just shook their heads. Old Rabbi Samuel said:

"And are you prepared to take the responsibility for the slaughter of thousands, my young man? No, if we are to survive we must let some of us die without a fight."

We did not dare to take the responsibility just then.

But the next evening news came to us that over one hundred and fifty persons escaped from the deportation center through Dzika Street into the open city of Warsaw. A German poster warning against such acts in the future blamed a Jewish policeman for the act.

Henryk did not return that night. He never came back at all.

During these first days of deportations, Michael, Daniel, and many other young people like ourselves printed leaflets that called at least for passive resistance. But my people were so caught by fear on the one hand and false, feverish hopes on the other, that no one would listen. They seemed deprived of will power and incapable of action. The Gestapo carried on its bestial task.

We Jews did not possess arms. Deportations continued.

Old Chaim and wrinkled Anna left quietly one morning.

"Goodbye, my little one. It is better that we should go," old Chaim said. "If it will spare you or others like you, it is better. I pray that you should live."

I could not hide my tears and I kissed his hand. I thought that in those weeks of horror I had almost forgotten how to cry.

"God bless you," Anna said, and her lips trembled.

I held on tightly to Michael's hand, for he was all I had left, and I knew that I would lose him too, sooner or later, and I asked Almighty God why he had punished so gravely a people so devoted to His faith.

There were 400,000 of us; there are 40,000 of us now. The streets of the ghetto are still with the silence of fear, mourning, and death. The hangman rests, but he will return again. Only this time we shall not go patiently to our death!

The change has come slowly. With a gladdened heart I have watched it come. Almost all the elders are gone, and the workers and former students have created the Jewish Armed Resistance Organization. Michael has become one of its leaders. We have been able to establish closer contact with the underground Polish military organization. At first they refused us arms. But then . . . .

At the beginning of January 1943, a single peasant cart came in through one of the gates. Friedrich M., an S.A. guard, had turned the other way; at any rate, he did not seem to notice. We had long before then discovered that Friedrich had a price. We paid, and he closed his eyes.

The cart rolled slowly to our house on Mila Street, where it stopped, and the aged peasant who had been sitting in it jumped off with surprising swiftness and ease. He began to take potatoes out of the wagon, while our main door was opened slowly and cautiously. A few minutes later the peasant had disappeared.

In the dimly lit cellar Michael and Stefan N. of the Polish underground were holding a whispered conversation. The old peasant turned out to be a young man of about thirty.

I sat at the entrance to the cellar watching for any unwelcome passersby, and tried to hear snatches of conversation. Michael's whisper was sharp and clear. The other man seemed firm but his evasions were tinged with guilt.

"Slavery knows no degrees," Michael was saying. "We are all brothers facing a common enemy. Friends, let us have arms! You have seen thousands of us die, and you know what future awaits us. Let the invader pay for life, death for death! We *must* have arms!"

"It is a difficult thing for us to decide, Michael. We have heard your name mentioned by every man who has left the ghetto alive. Your legend grows and your people believe in you, I grant that. But do not expect too much from us. This is no time for us to strike."

"This is the only and the last time for us. It is our final reckoning. We do not ask you to fight with us or for us. We only ask that you help us regain our honor. We expect only the minimum—your sympathy and your arms. I have found a way to make bombs and hand grenades, and we have been preparing them secretly in the ghetto. But we need much more than that. How can you refuse us?"

I saw Stefan N. of the Polish underground bow his head. We knew the pressures upon him. We also knew that he represented the Polish Socialist Party; we had counted on their support. He now looked into

Michael's fiery eyes, his dark hair falling wildly over his forehead, and stretched out his hand.

"You shall have arms, Michael of the ghetto. More than that I cannot promise. From the Polish underground to the fighters in the ghetto, take this message. You shall have arms."

A gate in the northwestern outskirts of the ghetto, where once a week starvation rations were brought in, in the form of bread made with rotten flour mixed with plaster and rotting potatoes, became the lifeline that made our armed resistance possible. Concealed under the load of bread and potatoes were shotguns, revolvers, and hand grenades. There were Jewish hands to unload precious food, but there were also Jewish hands ready to receive weapons for the battle to come.

We might have been shadows staggering along the streets, we might have been weak, exhausted, hungry, and sick, but we dreamt of an armed encounter with the enemy. The fire of hatred and revenge burned deep within our hearts. And somehow, we knew now that the hangman had been afraid of our wrath. He had tried to tell us that the reports of gas chambers were not true. He had slaughtered us when our morale was broken—secretly, separately, in cowardice.

We, the Jews, were strong, for we were not afraid to die. Not any more. But we had determined that we would sell our lives dearly.

We prepared for revolt feverishly and with deadly efficiency.

They came for us on the night of April 19, 1943, the first night of Passover. First—the sound of boots. Armed German detachments surrounded the ghetto, then marched in to complete its liquidation. Many came in cars mounted with machine guns and in tanks.

I watched them from our hiding place. They were sure of themselves, as always, and seemed almost bored with their task. They had come to bring the final end to the meek, fear-stricken population of the Warsaw ghetto. But they had miscalculated, for we were neither meek nor afraid any longer.

I looked at Michael's wrinkled brow; he was deep in thought. He noticed my searching glance, and his hand went immediately to the gun at his belt.

"We are ready, my love. Do not be afraid."

The streets were empty, as the Germans soon found out. The ghetto stood silent as the grave.

But suddenly the roofs and seemingly unoccupied houses burst out with the vengeance of thousands. Our guns began to play.

At last we had opened fire on the enemy.

Instantly stunned, the Germans began to flee in confusion. Our sudden blow threw their forces into a panic. They were gone as quickly as they had come.

We had tried to meet them on the field of battle, and they had fled. Some of them were lying there, dead on the pavement of the Warsaw ghetto, as mortal as the thousands of us who fell in gas chambers at Oswiecim and Treblinka. or on those very streets.

We were strong with the strength of despair, courageous with the courage of the doomed. Our last battle had finally begun.

More dynamite and bombs were smuggled in. And the German tanks returned. They took severe punishment in those first days, for the flame of our wrath burned high. Hundreds of them were killed and wounded. Several times they had to retreat behind the ghetto wall.

Men, women, and children were fighting in our common battle with the intensity of unloosed slaves. We crawled toward German tanks with hand grenades, aimed our rifles straight at the despised Nazi uniforms, killed with amazing and prompt accuracy, killed to save the remnants of humanity within ourselves.

The response of the persecutor to his early defeats came soon enough. Incendiary bombs were dropped on us from the air; the Germans attacked with flame throwers and heavy artillery.

Cannons were posted in the streets around the ghetto—heavy machine guns were placed on the neighboring houses. Death rained down everywhere.

Michael was in the very heat of the fight, just as he had been the guiding hand of our preparations for it. He seemed to alight from every corner, every street and house, to bring a word of courage to the fighters and death to the invaders.

We did not try to spare each other. We had remained alive through a series of accidents. We had remained in love.

The Germans dared enter the ghetto itself only by daylight. During the nights they retreated, guarding the approaches to the ghetto and shooting constantly.

On April 23, they took the central and outer parts of the ghetto. The main battle then continued in the north. But we managed to maintain strong guerrilla activity even in the conquered parts. The burning in the main ghetto kept spreading. The fires were becoming intolerable, and the end seemed to draw closer for all of us.

On the fifth day of battle the Jewish Fighters' Organization issued an appeal to the non-Jewish population of Warsaw, but there was no answer to our call.

On the sixth day of the battle, when I had just returned from a corner of Niska Street after having taken its defenders more ammunition, I came across Michael and Daniel engaged in a feverish discussion in the cellar.

"The munitions depot on Okopowa Street must be destroyed. No two ways about it, Daniel."

"Michael, let me go. You have no right to trifle with your life, not just yet. The fighters need you more than they need me."

"I fail to see your logic, Daniel. I know the territory better than you, and I am more accustomed to the handling of explosives. We can't afford to miss this time. You are to leave with a detachment heading in the opposite direction. This is an order."

I did not want him to see my face, for I knew that this was the end. But I wanted so much to take one long last look at him that I came out of the shadows of the cellar.

"You're back," he said. And then he motioned to Daniel, who was staring at the floor, and said:

"It's time."

Daniel looked at us both.

"I wish you two had a chance," he blurted out. And then he left.

Michael inspected the gun at his belt. Then he picked up a small bundle of explosives from the gray stone floor.

"I must go," he said.

I did not answer him—I just stood there looking at his dark figure, and I did not want him to leave. There was a deep furrow around his mouth that I had not noticed in the fever of the last few days. He smiled at me just then, and his face lit up with a flicker of the old hope. Or so I must have imagined, for we both knew that there was no longer anything to hope for.

"It has been a good life because of you," he said impulsively. "I love you more than mere words can express."

No, I refused to accept the cruel verdict! I could not bear to touch him, for I might never have let him go. I turned toward the wall and embraced it with aching arms. He must have felt as I did, for he just walked past me up the stairs. I heard the door close, and I began sobbing wildly into the wall.

He died that same day.

I do not know how he died, and Daniel said only:

"He died heroically."

I could not ask how he died. I know that Daniel has told me the truth. In the dark days of my life afterwards I often repeated to myself:

"He died a hero. . . ."

A trite cliche? Perhaps. Yet it was the only thread that could bind me to reality, reconcile me to life.

For days following Michael's death I fought on in a blind fury, and existed only because of my terrible thirst for vengeance. Days became weeks, and still we lived and died and we fought on. At the close of the fourth week regular operations gave way to guerrilla warfare. The Jewish-German war, they called it in Poland.

At the end of the fifth week Red Cross ambulances were still evacuating German dead and wounded from the ghetto. When almost every house had been burned, and we had retreated underground to cellars and other passages, we issued our last appeal to the Allied nations. The last house in the ghetto had fallen, but the world did not hear our cry.

I do not know how I left the ghetto. Daniel would not tell me then. I had been unconscious, and now Daniel is dead. I suspect that he carried me through the underground passages, then through city sewers to freedom, at a terrible risk and hardship.

I awakened in a peasant hut a few days later with heavy wounds and a slight brain concussion. The peasant woman later delivered me to the Polish underground. Daniel was with me when I first awoke and he said:

"I promised Michael to save you if I could. . . ." And then he turned and left me. In the grip of a great fever I understood even then that he was going back to finish the fight.

The Polish underground sent me here to England as soon as I had recovered, for I was a queer specimen—one of the last remnants of a dead people.

Seven weeks after the battle of the ghetto began, guerilla fighting still went on among the ruins. The head of the S.S. and of the police in the Warsaw district, Von Sammern, was dismissed. Governor Fisher of Warsaw was also removed.

On a cold February day in London, in the year 1944, the commander-in-chief of the Polish army bestowed posthumously the silver cross Virtuti Militari, the highest military honor known in Poland, on engineer Michael S. of the city of Warsaw.

It was a mere gesture on the part of a government that had done nothing to help the fighters of the ghetto while there was still time. However, one must learn to be grateful even for gestures.

As the general read the citation I thought:

"Yes, Michael, you have been a truly great engineer. For you have built us that invisible passage for which I had hoped many months ago—the passage to immortality. Thousands of Jews have crossed the stormy waters into the unknown through your passage. They will rest in peace, for they died like men. The passage you built extends far beyond the unknown, into the pages of the history of the future. You have given us a glorious place in that future, among the soldiers of freedom, in the family of the United Nations, among those who died for a better world."

You might ask me how I can live without Michael. I do not know if there is a life after death, but I'll tell you how I live.

Michael has restored my national pride. I know now that my people are fighters and that I too must fight to the very end. "Why fight?" you might very well ask. "Are you not yet tired of fighting?" The answer is really quite simple.

To make another ghetto impossible for all the time to come, anywhere on this earth, for any people on this earth.

To break down walls greater still than those of the Warsaw Ghetto, the walls of injustice, prejudice, blind fanaticism, brutality, and inhumanity.

This I must do for Michael and for all those who lie buried forever beneath the vast rubble that was once the home of Warsaw's Jews.

I wrote "The Invisible Passage" when I was a college freshman in one of Dr. Brewster's writing classes; I believe that it was the first fictional piece on the subject of the Warsaw Ghetto written in the West. Although it received a prize in the late 1950s, it was not published until 1969, in a short story collection with the same title, The Invisible Passage. It was republished in a Berkeley magazine in April 1983.

A Room Not One's Own

The last few months had been difficult for Jadwiga Balicka. She had to move suddenly from Lodz to Warsaw, to face widowhood, and to adjust to a new job at the Ministry of Transport. She sighed, thinking of her late husband, Zenon, as the oddly new-looking replicas of ancient, freshly rebuilt Warsaw slid beyond the dusty windows of the streetcar. He had been so handsome in the spring of 1938 as they walked together in the Krasinski Park! She was half-afraid to look straight up at him, for he might guess the veiled secret of even her vaguest longing. She stumbled, her university texts tumbling to the sidewalk, and he caught her hand. Chagrined by such clumsiness she let him lift her up to her feet, and for a breathless moment confronted his steely blue eyes.

"Father Szymanski says it's better to marry than to burn," he blurted out. "So let's get married because I am burning to a crisp."

She smiled faintly, as she had then, at that startling proposal. A wisp of sentiment, a memory so tenuous, so swiftly gone. The forces of war and conquest cared nothing for the promises of tenderness and the expectancies of love. The bombs exploded, the country surrendered, all life had turned to refuse a year later. Zenon joined the underground, to the tugging apprehension in her heart. Would tonight be their last, she wondered constantly. In her ears burned again the plaintive siren of the Gestapo; she heard the nocturnal banging on a door nearby.

But Zenon had survived. Peace came and they were together still, even if nothing else would ever be the same. Then seven years after the war had ended, he was killed in a Lodz factory accident. "Pray to the Virgin Mary, Pani Jadziu," advised a neighbor. Despite all the party propaganda to the contrary, her contemporaries filled the churches to overflowing, but she could find no such comfort. She had misplaced her once deep faith somewhere between the first and the last salvos of Nazi artillery that had systematically leveled Warsaw in the 1944 uprising.

She raised her hands to her eyes, trying not to think of it, not to remember. But the memory overpowered her will. She lay in a coal cellar once more, giving birth prematurely to a tiny girl, while over her head clanked the echoes of the city's cruel annihilation. Her best friend, Genia Pawiak, had cut the umbilical cord with a pair of unsterilized scissors. Zenon was somewhere with the Home Army, hanging onto streets, buildings, retreating by inches. Across the Vistula were Soviet troops, immobile though poised for attack. The Home Army's orders had come from Poland's London government-in-exile, and the Russians would not lift a rifle to help. The city was burning. The infant breathed for a moment, and died.

So by the time the factory director delivered Zenon in pieces to her in a plain pine box she possessed only tattered fragments of her Christian upbringing, not enough for even a single prayer. She thanked her neighbor politely for her advice. She would leave Lodz, she decided abruptly. Genia had a decent position at a government ministry in Warsaw—the city had been rising from the ruins. They needed people, she kept writing. With their background, why did Jadwiga and Zenon insist on immersing themselves in the idiocy of a provincial town? She had never told her friend of the grilling Zenon had received at the Ministry of Security about his Home Army connection. Yes, she would go to Warsaw now that Zenon was no more and his suspect political past had been laid to rest with him in his grave.

In the capital she found a temporary abode, a tiny room with her mother's old friend, Anna Bronska, a retired school teacher, who to make ends meet—an impossible task—took in boarders. In Bronska's apartment she shared with five others a bathroom with constantly balky plumbing. She had her midday meal at the Ministry cafeteria and a snack there before going home. It would save her, when she had a place of her own, from getting up at five a.m. to stand in a queue for two hours to buy food. The Ministry had just been assigned a housing bloc for its employees. She would be transferred there as soon as her things arrived from Lodz and the minister had signed the necessary papers. Altogether as good a situation as one could expect.

When Genia triumphantly brought her a signed apartment requisition, she did not at first comprehend. She had glanced at the slip of paper with indifference; then, startled, raised her eyes to her friend's face. The address was a street in the old Jewish ghetto that had long since ceased to exist.

"But, Genia, do you realize where this is?"

Genia avoided eye-to-eye confrontation. She spoke quickly, far too quickly.

"You don't know how lucky you are. It's the last vacancy in the whole complex. I managed a transfer there myself only last month."

"You of all people? How could you live there?" The words were out of Balicka's mouth before she could choke them back. For Genia's Jewish lover, whom she had hidden in an armoire in her apartment the

first year of the German occupation, sick of being shut up, went voluntarily into the ghetto, from which he never returned.

"I'm not ashamed of it," said Genia defiantly. "We must forget the
past. What's finished is finished. One must live."

I suppose, thought Jadwiga, as the trolley halted before a new
housing bloc, Genia has the right attitude. What good were her own
ruminations about a past she could not alter? She got off and began
searching in her bag for the keys. She had moved into the apartment
that very morning, and had spent the day at the Ministry of Transport
filling out additional papers so that the place would be legally hers.
But looking after the trolley she again drew in her breath, as she had
for the first time when she had contemplated the long, graying bloc of
houses, perched at the edge of a vast ruin. Curtains had fluttered in a
first-floor, half-opened window. In another, someone had set out a box
of struggling red geraniums. Yet all this life-proclaiming normality
failed in Balicka's eyes. Why did they have to build it here?

She walked rapidly past the monument to the fighters of the ghetto.
The sculptor had pictured them as armed to the teeth, rifles and auto-
matics slung over their shoulders, their ammunition belts and leather
bags brimming with grenades. Their faces, young, clean, heroic, and
beautiful, were gazing toward the sky. Yet she knew for a fact that in all
of the ghetto there had not been a single rifle, only pistols and knives,
and that even grenades had been scarcer than bread. Zenon agreed
with the sculptor's version. This is how they ought to look to the
world, before the delegations that came to lay wreaths at their feet.

Yet she could not help remembering how it really was during that
Holy Week 1943. The last forty thousand Jews of the ghetto rose in a
doomed, final rebellion. The Germans retaliated, attacking with tanks,
fire bombs, and heavy artillery. While Warsaw celebrated the resurrec-
tion of Christ, the ghetto burned.

Zenon swore to her—again and again, for she would not believe
him—that the Home Army had given an order to break through the
ghetto wall near Bonifraterska Street, and that inside, Mordecai Anielewicz had received the message. Zenon said that his unit had waited for
those few who had straggled out through the sewers, covered with
slime and smelling horribly of excrement, more dead than alive. But
they failed in their attempt to dynamite the wall, and there were
corpses on both sides.

She had heard all too often from her compatriots, even in the
blackest days of the occupation and despite the hatred the Nazis en-
gendered, an echo of shameful relief. Sometimes it was plainly stated:

"They are doing the job for us so we won't have to. After all, the Jews have always constituted a foreign element in Poland." Because of such convictions a president, the bright hope of the country's future, had been assassinated in the 1920s. She wanted Zenon's unit to atone somehow for that murder and for all the others—for the denunciations to the Gestapo, and for the grisly implication of a Christian Poland's wishes, no matter how tentatively expressed.

Was it true, she wondered once more, what Zenon had told her? Had they really tried?

How many lay buried forever beneath the rubble and ashes of the wasteland that stretched out beyond the housing bloc? She shuddered, took the keys from her bag, opened the heavy downstairs entrance, and ran, breathlessly, up to the third floor. The elevator, as in so many of the new buildings, was out of order.

Her new quarters had a Spartan appearance. A bed, a small rug from Zakopane, three wooden chairs from a government-run native craft store, a miraculously preserved table that had belonged to Zenon's mother, a lamp, a pile of paperback books. A small pine table fitted into the alcove adjoining the kitchen. She would get some curtains, unpack the trunk that contained a few knickknacks and pictures, get some peasant cutouts at the craft shop. It would be something, it might even be all right. She rummaged among her things, found sheets, a pillow, a blanket. She leaned hard on the bed frame, moving it so that it would face a blank wall instead of the window, for the view was not one to cheer her heart. Outside darkness was falling quickly. She was so weary, and the bed was so beckoning. . . .

She awoke sometime later, certain that she was back in Lodz. From her bed, turned toward the open window, she could see curtains fluttering in the breeze. But . . . these were not the printed orange and blue cotton ones she had once made in an outburst of domesticity. No, these were Austrian tulle, but somewhat worn, as if they had seen better days. Beneath the window stood an antique chair, covered in green plush; an old-fashioned commode was against the left wall, its surface crowded with framed photographs. No, this was not her apartment in Lodz! As she shook herself further awake, she knew that she had never seen the room before and that none of the things she was gazing at had ever been hers. With this realization a feeling arose in her, an irresistible conviction, that someone was standing behind the kitchen door. She got up and immediately pushed it open. No one. She turned back to the room and noticed to her astonishment that in a corner squatted a tall, old-fashioned coal-burning blue tile stove, similar to one she remembered in a house on Nowy Swiat where she had lived as a child.

With shaking fingers Jadwiga groped next to the bed for her bag. In it was a bottle of sleeping pills prescribed following Zenon's fatal accident by a Lodz doctor. "I am not well," she thought, "and I am hallucinating." She swallowed one pill, then another. Sleep soon enveloped her.

The following morning she decided not to mention her dream to Genia as they both boarded the trolley car for the Ministry. She passed the monument without a glance and scrupulously avoided looking in the direction of the rubble beyond the housing bloc.

That afternoon she stood in line to get a few things, and was lucky enough to obtain three half-stale rolls, some condensed milk, and a box of English tea biscuits. By the time she entered the apartment, dusk was falling. She switched on the lamp with a white pleated shade that a cousin of Zenon's had sent her from America. Nothing inside had been disturbed, and the barren walls gave her renewed comfort. She ate a roll, boiled water for a spoonful of precious Nescafé she had saved in a small glass jar, added condensed milk, and stirred absentmindedly. She was grateful now to have this oasis of peace after a harried day of work for a very nervous assistant to a vice-minister. If there were enough hot water she would even take a relaxing bath.

Later that night the dream returned, with an identical sequence. She woke in a bed not her own, in a room not hers, facing a window instead of a wall, with the same curious feeling that someone else was present. She got up, inspected both rooms and all doors, found no one, took more pills, fell asleep again, uneasily.

The dream became part of her existence. She resigned herself to it as to the ringing of the alarm clock at six a.m. Apparently there was to be no let up in its repetition. If anything, the features of that other room grew stronger, clearer with the passing of time. Over the commode hung a mirror in a heavy ornamental frame of encrusted brass. Next to it she had begun to notice a portrait of a man with a shock of jet black hair, and another of a woman, leaning on her arm, over a table covered with books and letters. And always, with the vision came the sense that someone—perhaps the room's inhabitant, was hovering nearby, just beyond a door. But her repeated search always proved futile. All she encountered was her own pale reflection staring from the brassbound mirror that was not hers, in a room in which she felt herself to be an intruder.

She finally spoke to Genia over lunch at the Ministry cafeteria. "You know, I've been having this very strange dream"—and a description began pouring out of her. She saw that Genia, who had a slight heart condition, was growing very pale.

Jadwiga had half-expected Genia to contradict her, to tell her she was overwrought, nervous, that she needed to see a doctor at the government clinic. She wished that her friend would find reasons in the nightmares of her yesterdays for the hallucinations of her present. But Genia was strangely silent, then finally spoke.

"Manek's sister (Manek had been Genia's Jewish lover), the only one in their family who survived, came to see me last Sunday. She looked out of my kitchen window and said: 'Did you know that right here, just outside your window, was the Umschlagplatz? We had to report here, ten thousand of us a day. . . . And over there were the railroad tracks and the freight cars. . . .'"

"Jesus Maria!" came from Jadwiga, involuntarily. Genia seemed not to hear, and continued:

"Do you think they blame me, those poor souls?" I asked her.

"No," she replied. "You did what you could. If anything, Manek's spirit is watching over you."

That night Jadwiga's dream was particularly vivid. The green plush in the old armchair seemed worn yet familiar, and almost inviting. The commode had acquired a pair of old brass candlesticks. The moon hovered over the open window, the very window that in the morning did not exist. It illuminated its frame and the fluttering curtains. Its reflection was caught in a crystal bowl on top of the commode, between the photos. Then, just as she was reaching for another sleeping pill, the front door opened.

The momentary stab of fear—Jadwiga knew of the frequent robberies in the city—disappeared at the sight of her visitor, a young girl, dark-haired, slender, almost frail. There was not the slightest doubt in Jadwiga's mind that the girl was Jewish. She felt instinctively that the strange room in which she had been awakening night after night had at last found its long lost occupant.

The girl moved a few steps toward Jadwiga's bed, then halted. Each took measure of the other. The girl did not speak, but Jadwiga would have sworn that she could read her visitor's thoughts: "Ah, so you are here. . . ." And she began speaking to her rapidly, making excuses: "You see this is a new building, and the Ministry assigned me this apartment. . . ." The girl made a slight gesture with her hands, as if to calm her. "It's all right," the movement implied. She had just stopped by for a moment, simple curiosity. . . . And she began walking toward the window.

Something made Jadwiga leap from her bed and follow that wan figure. Oh, yes, she remembered the sound only too well, the staccato of an automatic and then a Molotov cocktail hitting the pavement, German curses, a cry of pain. She was standing at the window, alongside the girl. Below she saw a square, lit as if by daylight. An SS-man was lying on the pavement in a pool of blood. Two other soldiers crouched behind the edge of a building, setting a machine gun in position. From a window across the square came pistol shots. Jadwiga took three steps backward in a gesture of self-preservation. Then she heard it plainly—the familiar howl. Fire bombs were falling on the house and the square. Someone across the way was screaming horribly, as if being burned alive. The acrid odor of smoke reached her nostrils. Her hand, curled into a fist, rose to her lips. Panicked, she turned toward the door. What about the girl, she remembered, and looked back for her companion. The curtains lay in a heap on the floor. The girl was standing on the parapet, looking down. And before Jadwiga could speak, her visitor jumped—holding both arms aloft like a wounded bird—to the pavement below.

Jadwiga stifled a scream. At that very moment the moonlight that had been flooding the room fluttered and was extinguished. With it receded the sounds of battle and the smell of smoke. In the equally awful silence Balicka stumbled toward her bed. She switched on the lamp. A solid wall confronted her where, just moments earlier, the girl had flown downward. The plush chair, the tiled stove, the commode, and the mirror had vanished without a trace.

The dream did not return. Gradually much of the former ghetto was covered with new housing blocs.

"A Room Not One's Own" is a more contemporary Warsaw Ghetto story, and is juxtaposed here for comparison with "The Invisible Passage." It was written in 1984 and published in the magazine Agada.

Syngar, the Slave

"Gallia est omnes divisa in partes tres, . . ." wrote mighty Caesar about the Gaul he conquered, and in Gaul lies my land.

I haven't much time to think, for in a few hours they are to come for me, the civilized Roman citizens—my betters. They will soak my clothes and body in pitch, so that I may burn all the brighter. They will build a fire in the market square, and drag me through the streets of Rome with my hands tied behind my back and with heavy chains upon my feet, so that I may serve as an example to my fellow slaves. And there will be gathered in the market place all of those who look with contempt upon me, a slave—the free Romans who would not soil their hands with toil as my hands are "soiled"—the common people, the soldiers, and the fine and noble patricians carried in their litters by their slaves. Yes, they will all come to watch me burn and to enjoy it. For I, a slave, dared raise my hand against my master and dared to dream of making other slaves free. No, I haven't much time to think.

Just enough perhaps to close my eyes and see the green plains of Gaul, my land, and the faces of my fellow "barbarians" as we are called here in Rome, the faces seen so very long ago and nearly forgotten. The hard, set visage of the chieftain, the lovely one of his daughter, the kind, wrinkled face of my father, the wise man of the tribe, the young and hopeful countenances of my brothers and cousins. Long dead and long forgotten. For when does a slave have time to think of his loved ones, of his old ones! The whip lashes hard over his back, and the harsh voice of the overseer reminds him every minute of his waking day that he is worth keeping alive, living and feeding, only as long as he produces. Helpless, old, or sick he may die like an animal, or worse than one. Is it a wonder then that the slave's thoughts, when he can gather them up in a mind dulled by relentless labor, turn to freedom? Freedom for his brothers and for himself. But a short step separates these thoughts from deeds, and deeds from bitter punishment. And yet though we know the risk, we try again and again, we break the masters' tools and we run away, for man yearns to be free. Once in Gaul I was free.

I was a free man.

"We fought the Romans before and we shall fight them again," spoke the chief. The gathered assembly nodded.

"Aye, we shall fight them again."

"The young blood of Gaul will defeat the Roman legions!" shouted my brother with fire in his eyes.

"Aye! Aye!" the others agreed, and their weapons clashed. I glanced at my father and saw a worried look steal upon his face. He did not nod with the others, but watched them silently. His expression filled me with foreboding. For my father was a man wise beyond all nature, cleverer than any man I knew, and well respected by all for his knowledge. He had taught me much of what I knew—of the healing powers of herbs, of the stars upon the heavens, of the music of our language, and of the beauty to be molded from a hunk of clay. He told me about the Romans, of their achievements and of their society, which though much advanced over our own, built as it was upon slave labor, was a threat to our very existence. He had told me of the countless battles we had fought with them, and the thousands of our people in their captivity. I had learned to fear the Romans and not to regard them lightly. No, I did not like the look upon my father's face.

Soon after, I saw him withdraw from the crowd, and I followed closely in his footsteps. He did not acknowledge my presence, and I waited for him to speak.

"'Tis a sad day for Gaul that is dawning, son," he said after some time had elapsed. "We shall fight, for fight we must, but we shall lose, and all of Gaul will be lost, and all of us, in one way or another. The Romans are dispatching one of their best legions to finish us off, and we shall not be able to withstand them."

"But father, wherefrom such grim news?"

"Think of the runaway slave who died in my arms a short while ago. He fled from Rome. It was indeed a great feat he accomplished to come back to die in his land. He told me, and I have spoken of it to no one, nor shall you. Promise me."

"I swear it, father."

"Good. You and your brothers make ready, for the Romans shall be here soon. The way I count it, it will be at the next change of the moon."

It is not easy to hear one's own death pronouncement, and though I loved my father well, and respected his wisdom, I could not quite believe that all was as bad as he said. I was young and strong, I loved a girl—and wanted to live.

Deep in thought I came upon the house where she lived, Vallida, my own, my very own. It was a great log house, for it belonged to the chief, and to his father who had been chief before him. The men were not yet returned from assembly, and the horses and cattle grazed upon the wide pasture that stretched beyond the house, high into the hills. Vallida was standing right before the house, shading her eyes with her hand, and looking toward the way whence I had come. She was tall and fair-headed, as are all our women, but sweeter and fairer than any of them. She wore a suit of fine linen and a fur cloak, for she was the chief's daughter, and her mother his first wife.

"'Tis you," she said. "Where are the others?"

"They'll be along soon, I expect."

"What are they debating about at the assembly?"

"Military matters," I said lightly. "That is why womenfolk were not called."

"Will you come in for some porridge?" she said. "It's ready and steaming hot."

"If you shall serve it, I will."

She smiled and brushed a stray curl from her forehead.

"Come in and you may get your wish."

I followed her indoors. There was no one about. I sat on the wooden bench at the table, and when she brought in the porridge and a pitcher of milk, I said:

"Will you not serve me as well when I take you to wife?"

"Better," she replied.

I grasped her hand.

"Shall it be soon, Vallida, my fair one?"

"As soon as my folk give their consent. I think my mother is willing, and my father shall do as she says. Your father has entreated her well."

"And you? Are you willing as well?"

"Syngar, need you have asked that question?"

No, I knew I need not have asked. It was more in jest than in seriousness that I asked it. Or perhaps because I wanted to hear her say it again. I had loved and wooed her fiercely and long. And it was now understood between us that we should one day be man and wife. She knew that though many took unto themselves more than one wife, she would be the only woman in my house. And she, too, looked at no other man.

But now, gazing upon her graceful figure bent over the fire which she was trying to stir, I thought of yet another fire and danger which might touch her fair brow. It was of the distant rumble of the coming of the Roman legion, of blood and thunder, of war and defeat that I was thinking. My lovely Vallida, my beloved, my cousin—for she was also of my kin—not as the mistress of my house but a slave led away by the

Roman conquerors. The thought froze the blood in my veins and crazed my mind. I could not bear to think it.

"Why look you so violently about?" she spoke in a soft voice. "Is something troubling you, dear Syngar?"

"'Tis nothing, love. 'Tis nothing. Here come the others. Let us go to the threshold to meet them. The porridge was fine, and I thank you well."

They came before the change of the moon and with the clatter of spears. They struck like lightning, though we fought well and gave all. When they came upon us they did not find us unprepared, though they arrived before their expected time. Our spears had been sharpened, our swords were ready to be used, and our hands eager to use them. Together we had prayed to our gods.

"For our homes and our land," intoned the chief.

"For our wives and daughters," spoke my father.

"For our freedom!" shouted my brothers.

"For our very lives," I whispered.

We gathered our women and children together swiftly in the chief's house as soon as we perceived the dust of their coming. With our shields and spears we formed a barrier to protect them, and so we waited in stony silence.

They came upon us in a great body, shouting the cries of battle. We were swallowed up and covered with them as with vermin within but a short space of time, though we were fierce as beasts defending their young. I received a sharp blow on the head which threw me to the ground long after the battle had begun, but I came to my senses sometime afterwards. The ground was strewn about with bloody corpses. To the right of me lay the bodies of my slain brothers. The struggle was over. The Romans were breaking down the doors of the great log house. There were cries and shouting from within but soon that ceased, and when the doors finally came down, the soldiers looked in and quickly retreated in great fear and astonishment. I raised my head, then part of my body to get a clear look within, and I saw the floor of the house strewn with the lifeless bodies of women and children who had taken their own lives with the chief's many weapons.

"Vallida!" I shouted in agony and despair. "Vallida, answer me, Vallida!"

There was no reply. But the legionnaires heard my cry and quickly came to my side, with raised spears.

"He seems alive and healthy enough," said one of them to another. "Let us take him along with the others," said the second. They shoved me into a clearing behind the house where some of my kin stood dazed and forlorn. As we walked by we passed the lifeless body of my father.

It was a long, weary march to Rome. Some of us died on the way, for our conquerors had strong whips and no pity. I walked the distance as if in a trance, and could later remember but a small part of the journey.

All that had been my life was now dead, for even the gods could not stay the power of the sword. But my body stubbornly lived on, to be driven ahead listlessly with the others, to be used from now on by men stronger and more powerful than I. I knew but one thing throughout that long journey—I was now a slave to be bought for a few dinars and used until death as a tool is used until it too wears out.

I was sold at the market square along with many others. The man who bought me came in a handsome litter carried by many slaves. He drew back its silken curtain with a bejeweled hand when they came to a halt before us. I saw his white toga of exceedingly fine material. I could just perceive the edge of a red tunic showing beneath his outer garment. His feet were clad in exquisite shoes of red leather with white buckles.

The Roman looked well fed and exceedingly bored. He observed us with contempt from under half-closed eyelids, then pointed to three men in the group, including myself, drew out his purse, and called upon one of his slaves to give it to the man who had charge of us.

We were then quickly chained together and bid to follow the litter, under the watchful eye of one of our new master's slaves.

We followed the splendid litter through the streets of Rome, filled with many idle men, and passed great edifices and elaborate houses. I marveled at the beauty and skill with which these had been executed.

They far surpassed anything I had ever seen.

Then I caught the eye of one of the slaves carrying the litter, and though he did not speak I understood that he saw my thoughts. He smiled sadly, shaking his head. He seemed to be saying: What of it? What of this beauty and harmony and grace, when it was built upon the backs of such as I? And I saw the sweat which stood out on his brow and the strain of the muscles on his arms which carried the litter.

He was a tall man, with a finely featured face worth remembering, surrounded by a rich red beard. I took him for a Scythian, for as my father had once remarked they were in the habit of wearing such beards and were distinguished by flaming red hair. His forehead was clean-shaven, as were those of other slaves, and their brows were branded. They wore clothes of a heavy, crude material.

At last we came to a stop at a handsome carved stone and marble villa beyond the city, surrounded by fields and vineyards, whose windows looked out on the sea.

In the garden the fountains murmured softly, and multicolored peacocks walked proudly among the marble benches and ornamental trees.

It was nearly nighttime, and dusk was falling slowly upon all that beauty and quiet. Our master disembarked from his litter, and without giving a glance in our direction entered the house.

Soon another man came toward us, dressed in crudely woven cloth and armed with a lash. He looked us over coldly. Suddenly his lash whistled, stinging our backs.

"So that we understand one another, and who is master here and who a slave," he said.

We were then led into our quarters some distance from the villa. The building was small, dirty, and ill-kept. Our heads were quickly shaved, our foreheads painfully branded. We went to sleep on pallets spread over the stone floor along with some twenty other slaves already there.

A new slave freshly in bondage does not sleep soundly, nor does he fall asleep with ease. And so I lay alongside my companions, listening to their uneven breathing, and could not close my eyes. I fancied that I saw the shadow of a human form moving along one of the walls. It seemed to crawl steadily though slowly toward me. It came close to me at last and I saw that it was one of my master's old slaves. The man touched me lightly on the shoulder and spoke in a whisper.

"Speak you the Roman's tongue?" he asked.

"Aye. My father was well versed in it and he taught it to me."

"And where lies your land, friend? Who are your people?"

"My land is in Gaul, my people a village tribe. They are no more."

"Our slave lot is not far different, Gallus, my friend. All the Roman masters are much alike."

"Who are you? And what is your name?" I said.

"A slave like you, and what I was before. . . . No need to think of that." The man grew stiff and still as though I'd opened a long forgotten wound, and then he said: "My name? I've forgotten that, as you no doubt shall forget yours. We have no use for names here. They call me the Nubian for I come from African shores. I am a strong and healthy man and a most valuable slave."

As he said the last words he flashed a smile that though it should have been bitter was not. And by the scant light that fell through the small opening close to the ceiling of our hut, I perceived that my companion was a handsome as well as an interesting man.

"Your lot here will not be of the worst," he went on. "You will work from before dawn to the full of night, and break your back at the plow and the stone. You will be chained, and whipped, and fed the scraps from the master's table, but your lot here will not be of the worst. You might have been sold into the mines, where you would have to dig deep underground for ore, and never see the sun. You might have been sold for the galleys, where your back would always be bent to the oars, and your head never raised up to see the sea and sky. You might have been put to work constructing high bridges of stone, building tunnels, draining lakes. At each of these occupations you would die within the year, or two or three. Here you have a good chance of living ten, perhaps fifteen years. Our master is a farmer, you see. That is, with our help."

"You speak as a friend," I said, "and in your mockery I perceive a spirit that will not bend or die. Take my hand, Nubian, for the Roman is our common enemy and you are my friend."

We clasped hands and sat silently for a moment. Then he spoke again:

"Watch out for the overseer. He has a nasty temper. Do not speak to me or the others when he is about. The work will go hard with you at first, but you will grow accustomed to it, have no fear. If you're in much difficulty in turning a stone or tying up the vines, just give me a look, and I shall try to help you if I can. My skin is black, so you can't mistake me. Now try to sleep—it will soon be time to rise."

He moved away noiselessly, and weariness overcame me at last.

It was still dark when I heard the shouting. The slaves were stirring all around me, and from the outside came the clatter of chains and the hoarse voice of the overseer.

The Nubian had spoken truthfully and well. We were chained and led into the fields, where we worked under the hot sun until the end of the day. Some of us pulled heavy plows, others lifted stones to clear the land, still others worked the earth with sharp instruments to prepare it for cultivation.

It was heavy labor, and sweat poured easily from our faces and bodies. We could rest but little. I had not much time to observe the others, for the whip of the overseer lashed freely when the work slackened. But I saw that my visitor and friend of the night before was a man of great stature and powerful limbs who led all the others in the performance of his work. The overseer's lash rarely whistled in his direction.

We did not speak to one another all that day, but I watched him carefully and tried to follow what he did. Other slaves toiled alongside us. The red-bearded Scythian pulled the plow until the muscles upon his back stood out sharply and glistened with sweat in the harsh and unrelenting blaze of the sun. His face was expressionless and he did not look toward me. We toiled in silence.

It was already dark when we returned to our hut and were given a meager meal. I ate it ravenously, though my whole body ached with the first day's labor and I longed to stretch my limbs upon the stone floor. There was a sore place on my back where the lash had fallen several times during the long day. I hadn't a thought in my head but to get some rest, and so I fell heavily upon the floor and instantly went to sleep. The Nubian did not come that night.

It was only after a week of backbreaking labor and nights of death-like slumber that I began to gather my senses once more and to think on the hopeless and despicable life before me, with each day just like the others, and all the days so closely resembling the life of the tamed beasts we had kept in Gaul. And in my despair I thought of escape, for I felt that I could not bear my fate.

It was then that the Nubian came to me once more. And it was as if he had been reading my thoughts, for he said:

"I know of what you are thinking for I have been watching your face. Don't do it, friend. You do not know the land nor anyone in the countryside. They will catch up with you in a few hours and beat you like a dog. You might live through the beating, and you might not. For though it is true that the master does not like to destroy his own valuable property, a runaway slave is a bad risk and almost worthless. No one will buy him, and if he stays on he may run away again. So to kill him is almost better than to keep him alive. And who can tell, Gallus, there might come a day when your chances will perhaps seem better than they are at present. It may be more wise to be patient, my friend."

Though it was hard to part with my one desperate hope, I saw the reason in his speech. I did not argue, but instead asked him of his former life, and was told of the African village from where he came, and the wondrous tools they had used for working the soil in that village, and of his people who were joyful and loved to sing as they labored, of the wood carvings they made, of the hunting they had done, and the sorrow and the strength and the love, and the laughter and the tears, and the dancing on feast days, and the mourning when death struck, of the going and the coming, of the living, and the loving, of the fighting and dying they had done. And I listened in great astonishment and wonder and admiration for it was truly a great tale, wonderfully told. As he neared the end I thought of my own people, and longed for my past life, as I knew the Nubian must have longed for his own.

The bearded Scythian had a voice that was deep and beautiful. When he sang about his people we all listened with heads bowed, and even the overseer kept his lash to himself. But he did not sing very often. He was a good man and a sad one. We talked in the evenings as we ate our daily ration of food. And we found ways to speak to one another while we worked and while we lay in our hut at night. Slowly I came to know the others, too—tall Germans, dark-haired Egyptians, and olive-skinned Greeks. It was not hard to be their friend, for we all shared a common fate.

The kinsman with whom I had been sold was a young lad and had never been strong. He toiled in misery by day and cried at night. He was whipped more often than I, and when I could I tried to relieve him, though the opportunity for that presented itself rarely. My own muscles had tightened and grown, my strength and health were good, but my kinsman did not fare nearly as well. When I watched him I often remembered how he had loved to sit at the great house of the chief's on many an evening and listen to the elders who spun tales about our past. I was but a few years his senior and the difference between us was not great, though I had already felt myself a man while he was still a child. And now we were both men in the eyes of our Roman master, though I bore well under the heavy strain and my kinsman was breaking under it.

One day he could lift his spade no longer. That day was very hot, and sweat poured from us all. It had rained heavily during the night, and the ground was wet and soggy. The overseer was in an ill temper, for the master, it seems, had not been satisfied with the product of our labor. The returns from the vineyard had not been what he had expected, and he let the overseer know that if things continued so he would soon be replaced by another. The lash thus fell most often on the back of my kinsman, who was the weakest and slowest of us all. I gritted my teeth in mute anger. Finally I saw the young man fall onto the muddy ground. He did not get up. The overseer was quickly at his side, cursing and kicking at his body. My kinsman did not move. The whip fell upon his arms, his back, and his head, again and again. I heard a piercing cry of pain, and then I lost my reason. For I fell upon the overseer, despite my chains, and with my bare hands tore the whip from him in wild fury.

I bent over my kinsman. His eyes were closed, and I could not see whether or not he was breathing. The overseer screamed, and from the distant house came the farm manager, house slaves, and finally the master himself, all running in our direction.

I was soon overpowered, heavily whipped, and put in chains for the night as well as for the day. All the other slaves also received a whipping, though not as harsh as mine, for they too were heard to grumble and to threaten.

My kinsman was left in the field. They picked up his body the next day and buried it far up in the hills. I was chained in the hut when they did this, and learned of his death from the Nubian. I wept then, for I remembered how many times he had sobbed at night from too much work, the pain in his bones and the longing for his past, and how I could not help him.

Many months thus passed and I ceased to count them all. The Nubian had taught me the Roman calendar, but I had no use for it. One day was much like another, one month much like any other month, and so I lost track of time. I took my daily beatings as I took my daily ration of bread, and I worked and went on living. I even thought of other things sometimes, though not very often. The Nubian worried about me but I was numb to his persuasions. Of late I did not even care to talk.

One evening as I sat outside our hut in my chains, I felt no hunger. I put aside my bread. There was no one about. I gazed around me, and my eyes fell on a small bit of red clay, softened by the rain of the day before. Soon my fingers touched it. I scooped up a little in my hand—it felt as it had in the old days. Before I knew what I was doing I began to shape an object between my fingers. It did not take long, for my old skill had not been forgotten, but the result was sad when compared with what I had once been able to create. It had shape and the lines were not bad, though the clay was wet still, but it had no soul, for I had felt no joy while making it. It stood there now, a vase that my fingers had fashioned. I looked at it and it looked at me. I heard voices just then, a little way off from the road that led toward my master's villa.

One of them was saying:

"Come along, Marcellus, let us look at the slaves' quarters. I haven't seen them here for a long time, too long in fact. It gives one the necessary lift, you know."

"Our tastes are different then, for I do not long to see them. They remind me of our shame."

"You amuse me, Marcellus. If I myself did not know you for a patrician and a cousin to Anastasia I would take you for one of the rabble, judging from the way you speak. Although even the rabble know better than that. Come now, I want to see what our glorious Legions are fighting for."

"Not for glory. you can be sure of that, but for dinars, my friend."

The voices were drawing closer, and I looked for a place to hide my vase and my person. Our second overseer was just returning from the fields; we had acquired him since the incident of my kinsman's death. He fell upon me with great shouting, and began beating me as he was accustomed to do whether it was day or evening. Then his eyes fell upon my vase, as I knew they must sooner or later, and he began to laugh hoarsely.

"Now what is this, you Gallic swine? You must be truly strong and able to find time and energy for this! Tomorrow you shall work a little harder in the field so as to have no strength for such idleness!"

He turned to the vase to kick it into little pieces, when a shout came from the road and stopped him.

Two Romans in white togas stood at the gate. Both were men of about thirty, cleanly shaven and handsome. One had an exceedingly high forehead and a faraway look in his eyes. It was he who had called to the overseer.

"What is the trouble?"

The overseer stepped aside humbly and revealed me fully to the visitors.

"The man is lazy, Master Marcellus," he said. "Look at the things he finds time to occupy himself with instead of doing honest labor." He pointed to that unfortunate vase standing at my feet. I averted my eyes for I cared not to look upon the Roman.

"Well well," said his companion. "What have we here? An artist? This is a good jest indeed. I am more amused than I expected to be. So we conquer artists of great talent, not only barbarians. Ha ha! Our Legions are more glorious than I thought!"

"Not all the art in the world is of Roman origin," said the first man quietly.

He came closer, bent down, picked up the vase at my feet and examined it. Then he looked at me. I looked at him, too, and did not mind his gaze though I had been ready to hate him as surely as I despised the other.

"Do you speak our language?" he asked.

"Ay!"

"You are an educated man?"

"A barbarian," I said.

He smiled. And then he said:

"I wish to show this to someone. Will you allow me to take it?"

"It is yours."

"I thank you."

"Come now, Marcellus," said the other. "You aren't serious about this ugly piece of clay, are you? It is crude and slave-made. What would you want with it?"

"It is my business," said Marcellus sharply. "Come now, Anastasia is waiting."

They left without another word. The overseer gave me an evil look and pushed me inside the hut. But he whipped me no more that evening.

It was not long afterward that I was summoned somewhat grudgingly by one of the house slaves to aid in his work in the master's own garden. When the overseer objected, the slave merely said:

"Mistress Anastasia's own orders." And he led me away.

It was a pleasant garden, quiet and peaceful. I worked and listened to the music of the rippling fountains. There was no heavy voice of the overseer, and no sign of a whip; it was a place for meditation. I had little time to reflect upon this strange turn of events before I heard the rustle of a woman's fine garments and saw a lady, tall and stately, resolutely striding in my direction. There was a look of thoughtfulness around her eyes which I liked.

She spoke to me at once and without hesitation.

"Are you the Gallus who fashioned the vase of clay now in my possession?"

"Ay."

"It is a thing of beauty. Do you know it?"

"The lady is too kind."

"Can others of your tribe fashion things as beautiful as that? And you, yourself? By what accident of nature were you able to create this perfect object?"

"My lady," I said, and anger rose up within me like a cloud. "'Tis only a Roman could speak words like these in a great conceit. For where if not from Greece and Egypt and India and other lands come the works of worth and beauty that make a Roman's life comfortable and full of ease? Oh, I know it all, for my father was a learned man who traveled and saw much and taught me all he knew. There are other lands besides Rome, and other peoples of talent.

She was silent for a long moment, and I perceived that I had disconcerted her. Finally she spoke:

"Perhaps there is something in what you say, Gallus, and I spoke too hastily. I see that I have hurt your sensibility. But tell me then, if other peoples are as great as we, and you are not a barbarian but an educated man, how is it then that we are the masters and you the slaves?"

"Because mastery of the sword transcends all other skills, it seems. And you have that. And numbers too. And the will and the desire to conquer, plunder, and enslave. We are but a peaceful people who till the land. Though perhaps we should have been more warlike so as to have learned better the art of war. And maybe one day we shall."

"Your talk does not quite carry conviction for me, Gallus. I do believe there must be an inherent weakness and inferiority in nearly all the people of this earth save the Romans. Or else we would not be so vastly superior in every field of human endeavor."

"Are you, my lady?"

I was bold but she did not seem to mind.

She paused and touched a flower with her hand.

"My cousin Marcellus speaks somewhat as you do, Gallus. That is strange."

As she turned to leave she said:

"You may come to work in my garden from time to time. And sometime if the Muse should inspire you again, perhaps you shall make me another thing of beauty."

And she was gone.

It was only long after she left that I realized I had just held my first long talk with a Roman who did not spit upon me nor use a whip to humble my person. It was a good feeling yet tinged with bitterness somewhat. For even she, a kind and educated woman, did not consider me, a Gallic slave, an equal to her own countrymen. I pondered this, and did not notice the approach of my master.

A voice cold and sharp as metal brought me back to my labor. The master had a frown upon his brow and wore a sour look around his mouth and nostrils.

"Get going, slave," he said. "See to your work or punishment will swiftly overtake you." He gathered up his clothes so as to keep them from any accidental contact with mine, and passed me by. I heard him call to one of the house slaves for wine, though it was full day and the sun showed no sign of inclining toward the West.

For many days afterwards I toiled with my fellow slaves in the fields belonging to our master, which stretched far beyond where our eyes could reach. The vines bore fruit, and we cared for it and finally picked it and carried it upon our backs. Then we made wine by treading upon the fruits with our bare feet and poured it into large jugs. These were taken away I knew not where. The German was caught eating some grapes and he was whipped severely. A slave from a nearby Roman household escaped, was caught, thrown in the dungeon, and later killed. I could now see more clearly how right the Nubian had been.

My heart desired freedom no less. If anything, I yearned more than ever to break my chains! But different thoughts began to occupy my mind. I looked at my fellow slaves. They were good men, though bent by heavy labor. Their backs bore the scars of many beatings; their hands were calloused by years of toil. They were sad and without hope.

Thinking of them I conceived of an idea that would embrace us all. If I could dream of freedom for myself, then why not for them as well? Did they not have the feelings that I had? Did they not come from lands and people for whom they yearned? Were not their lives as precious as my own? And was not one slave another slave's brother?

I spoke of this to no one, not even to the Nubian, who was closest to my heart. When the red-bearded Scythian sang his strange and beautiful songs, I perceived in his voice the longing that was my very own— and that of all of us, all slaves. It was a longing for a land far away, for our kinfolk perhaps, for a woman we held dear, for the right to toil on our own land. I watched the bent backs of my brother slaves, the faraway look in their eyes when the Scythian sang, and within me grew a hatred of the Romans greater than I had ever known before.

It was the bloated face of our master and his body soft and heavy with easy living and too much good food that I compared with the lean bodies of my comrades—his soft ringed fingers with their rough ones.

I thought of Anastasia too, and though I could not equal the measure of hatred I held for her husband I did not and could not forgive even her. For she too was a part of it all. Did she not live off the sweat of our backs? And did she consider us men?

Thus I grew bitter in my thoughts. But I grew stronger too, for now these thoughts were of more than one human being in chains: they were of all human beings sharing a common fate.

Thyrsis, a Greek slave whose main task was the care of our master's clothes and body, once more came to fetch me at my labor.

It was grain threshing time, and sweat stood upon our brows.

"Come quickly, Gallus," he said. "You shall help us at this evening's feast, and the master's friends are many. Soon they will begin to arrive, and we must make ready for them."

They came in many splendid litters carried by slaves. Upon a large long table within the villa stood gleaming goblets of wine and silver dishes piled up with food. The guests lounged upon the couches with wreaths of flowers on their heads. The dishes were varied and plentiful, the like of which I had never seen before. It was a sight for one so often hungry, and afterwards when all lay in a drunken stupor around the table—and some beneath it—I stole leftover morsels of food.

There were some handsome men among those present, and several of the women were of great beauty. I had been chosen to fill their goblets with wine as swiftly as they were emptied, and had to work with great speed. Thyrsis was overseeing the food and wine while a number of other slaves moved back and forth to see to the comfort of the master's fine company. About ten slaves held lit candles and stood motionless about the hall.

One of the guests had a luther, and he played it with much skill. He sang verses too, which spoke of Roman gods and did not please me well. There was much laughter and talk about hunting, music, philosophy, and love. I was treated as if I were but one of the stones in the floor on which the couches stood.

It was incredible how much they drank. We in Gaul were men too and drank our wine as men should, but never to such an excess. The women drank along with the men, and they too fell into a drunken stupor at the end of it all.

It was toward the end of this merrymaking, while my master lay upon his couch with his eyes closed, his hands around the neck of a beautiful raven-haired girl, Anastasia having retired sometime earlier, that I was able to lean against one of the pillars that supported the ceiling of the hall. I too closed my eyes, and thought upon all that I had seen that night. I hated the Romans—yet I envied them. I envied them the right to do with their lives as they pleased, not the kind of lives they led. I would have done much differently with mine had I the liberty to do as I wished. I did not envy them their sordid pleasures, but their freedom that I envied so!

A gentle tap upon my shoulder gave me a sudden start. In a beautifully draped toga, slightly shaky and with a sadly mocking smile upon his lips, stood Marcellus, whom I had not seen all evening.

He shook his head and pointed toward the drunken scene before us.

"Look well, Gallus," he said. "Look thee well. There lies Rome—gorged, satisfied, bloated, victorious—and asleep. That is how it usually celebrates its superiority and its victories. And that is how it shall perish—drunken and asleep."

"And yet, though asleep, you are strong," I answered him. "Stronger than this and mightier," and I bared the muscles of my arm. Marcellus touched them with his long soft fingers and laughed.

"Ah, but we are growing flabby and soft. Julius Caesar took eight hundred of your towns in ten years, subdued three hundred tribes. He killed a million men and brought back another million as slaves. And yet today, our legions cannot hold the conquered lands. There are stirrings from one end of the empire to the other. The plebeians are grumbling, for they have forgotten how to work and must live off the crumbs we throw them."

And then, leaning heavily upon my arm, he said in softer tones:

"Gallus, my friend, for thou shall be my friend, I feel my world is perishing, and I do not care. I never liked it much. I do not wish to live upon your blood, and yet I do not know how to live otherwise. And that is why I hate this world of mine, for while it has made me a part of itself it has also made me hate my own self for being a part of it."

"It is not often that a slave hears such words from one of patrician origin," I said. "But even when I saw you first I thought that you must be an honorable man, though I shrank from believing that it was so. I see in you compassion for one like myself. You treat me like an equal, and I am grateful for that. And now I wish to ask you man to man. Are there no Romans in this powerful city who speak and feel like you? Are there no more who hate the enslavement of others? Tell me, are there no more?"

"What is thy name, Gallus?" he asked me first.

"I've nearly forgotten. Syngar is my name."

"Syngar, my friend, there are not many more. And those who feel thus are afraid to speak for they shall be banished or killed for taking up the cause of slaves." He paused.

"There was a man in Rome," he went on, "who was a teacher of the young. He once said of our circuses, where prisoners and martyrs are devoured by wild beasts, and where gladiators are made to fight unto death, thus: 'Man is driven by whips and fire to fight with his fellow man. . . . Romans, do you not see that evil will befall those who are responsible for these cruel crimes against your fellow men?' Yet none listened to him."

"He taught that slaves are people like ourselves, that they are human beings, and that all people in the world are brothers. Do you not think so, Syngar?"

"It is difficult for me to feel that the Roman is my brother, though knowing you has changed my mind somewhat. Perhaps if they would all pay heed to that teacher you speak of they might become more like you. Until then, all men in chains are my brothers, and all free men who live by their own toil, and those who stir against the Roman masters, they are my brothers too."

He grew sad and bade me walk with him into the garden. The moon was bright, the fountains murmured softly, and flowers smelled sweet and enchanting.

"Right is on your side, Syngar. You have seen through me and through the old teacher as well. For though we speak big words and utter noble thoughts, we have no courage to break our own bonds or to aid you in breaking yours. We choose not to fight but to bear all stoically. In consequence, that is all that we can offer you as counsel and advice."

We passed a bench beautifully made of Parian marble and a statue of golden bronze. Its beauty brought back the somewhat bitter memory of my only conversation with the mistress Anastasia.

"This house, this garden, this land, made and tilled by slave hands," I said. "I as a slave know my capabilities, yet even an enlightened Roman like your fair cousin does not give the barbarian his due."

His face lit up in a smile.

"Anastasia?" and he said it like a caress. "She is but a flower poisoned by the evil weeds growing all around her, but she is still the brightest flower of them all." The smile vanished and I saw a great shadow come into his eyes. I had touched upon something that hurt and troubled my friend.

"I, a slave," I continued, "have learned many things. But how to break my chains I have not learned yet—although someday I will."

"I know that day is coming," said Marcellus. "I know that thus will come my end. I do not look forward to it for I am a doomed man. There is hope for you but none for me, and yet I wish you well. I cannot tell you to do as I do, which is nothing save idle talk. But I cannot at the same time help wishing for my heart's peace that you too should remain a stoic, well though I know that it is all but impossible."

He seemed weary and spent.

I left him sitting upon the marble bench and went in to help the other slaves carry their masters to their litters. The night was drawing to a close.

Many months afterwards I woke one morning and did not find the Scythian by my side. We were accustomed to sleeping next to one another, separated by but a small patch of straw. That morning, however, the Scythian was not there. I had been troubled by dreams that night. The day before, I had seen Marcellus in my master's garden. He had spoken of great stirrings among the slaves. The conquered peoples too were rising. The tribesmen of Gaul and Germany had turned their arms against Rome, and the Romans were hurling their legions from one end of the empire to another.

Strange things were happening within my breast when I listened to his account. All over Rome the breasts of other slaves must have held similar feelings when they heard. Within us moved a new power, a great yearning to be free. We raised our heads to listen to the sound of arms clashing in the north; we straightened our backs a little and clenched our fists.

The Scythian was not at my side. My eyes, accustomed to darkness, saw all the others—the Nubian, the Greeks, the Germans. He alone was missing, and my pulse beat faster for I had a strange feeling that I would not see him that day.

They spotted his absence shortly after we went out into the fields. We were dragged back for a flogging and questioning, but none knew what had happened to our golden-voiced comrade. Or none cared to tell. Men were dispatched in search of him, and dogs were sent to follow his trail. We heard their furious barking high in the hills.

They brought him back the following morning, bloodied, his clothes torn, his face tired and hopeless. He did not look at us nor did he utter a word. Toward evening the master ordered a stake rigged up before our very eyes and had the Scythian tied to it with heavy cords. The overseer lit the fire then, and all of us, chained together, were brought to witness the punishment. The flames licked the pile of wood slowly at first, then faster and faster until they reached his clothing. It is then that he began to sing, and his voice went through the very insides of our being. It was a melody, not sad, but defiant, and it fired the blood in my veins. The Nubian covered his eyes. The lash fell swiftly upon his back. The master's orders were that we all watch until the end.

And so we did—until the last breath and last note died upon his lips, and something inside of us died too. And something new was born.

None of hesitated, none wavered now. Our hearts were filled to the brim with hatred. We had come to the end of our endurance. Even the Nubian shook his head in agreement.

"We are together now," he told me. "And that is how it should be. To be alone is to be caught before one ventures out. There is strength in numbers."

Weeks passed while we prepared. The Nubian secured a blunt instrument to cut our chains, and drew maps of the countryside, which he knew well. We concealed some of our working tools behind the shed where we slept. From conversation with Marcellus I learned the location of city gates.

We awaited our day with bated breath.

It came when one of the overseers went into the city with some of the master's produce. Anastasia was at the house of a friend.

We struck before dawn. First we cut our chains. Then we divided into three groups. Several Greeks and two Germans took care of the other overseer with the aid of our work tools.

The Nubian and I headed for the house. We moved quietly and with care. The fountain shimmered in the moonlight. The flowers inclined their heads. Peace reigned over the household.

The Nubian overpowered the house servants and slaves one by one. It was all done quietly and with expert care. Not one of them knew what was happening to him, nor did any have time to warn the others. Several joined us. We killed only one, Pallianus, the most vicious and hateful of them all. The others were tied together and given over to a third group that waited outside. They were taken into our shed, far enough from the house so that even if their mouths should become unbound no one would hear them. Some of us kept watch over the shed.

We entered the master's bedroom quietly. I struck him a blow across the head with one of my tools. It was a fitting death. From the strength of my hands and from my toil the master had lived. It was from a blow delivered by those very hands that he now died.

It dawned when we set fire to the house. A wanton act, perhaps, but to us it was meaningful. Thus we destroyed all that bound us to our lot. We burned our master as he had burned the Scythian.

Then we left. Each of us had taken the clothes that belonged to the master's servants, and we separated. If we got out alive we would meet beyond the city gates. We could then plan our next moves. We were armed with tools concealed beneath our garments.

The Nubian and I stayed until everyone had gone. We watched the house burn to the ground. Ashes covered the lovely fountains and the flowers. We looked at each other then for perhaps the last time, threw our arms around each other's neck, and wept unashamedly.

"Goodbye," said the Nubian. "Perhaps we shall meet again. Perhaps not. If we are caught, we shall have to die. I have no fear of death. But no matter what, we have this to remember! We have broken our chains with our own hands. No one can take that away from us. Luck be with you! Farewell, my friend!"

I made my way cautiously into the city. I passed imposing edifices without half seeing them. The streets were already full of plebeians, who for want of something better to do argued with one another or followed the litters of their patrons. I felt them looking at me and I grew worried. I hoped I did not look too much like one unaccustomed to the freedom of the streets. Although I felt all eyes upon me, I steadied myself with the thought that every fugitive feels in danger of recognition even when there is no reason for fear. Slowly my breath grew normal, my eyes less wild, my step firm. I even stopped seemingly to listen to some gossip on the way. Yet I felt my new-won freedom hard to bear, and I prayed to the gods of my youth to see me safely away from Rome with all its glitter and beauty.

I could not have been very far from the city gate when I saw him, and I saw him too late. Walking directly toward me was my master's other overseer, who had gone to town on the master's business the previous day. It was too late to turn or run away. He recognized me at once and raised a great cry. In a moment I was surrounded, and though

I fought like an animal I was beaten to the ground and overpowered. Then my hands were tied behind my back.

Lying in the dungeon and waiting for death—as many have done before me and many shall have to do yet before freedom is won—I have had time to reflect.

It is said that a man's whole life passes before him in the last hours and moments of his existence. So has mine, the good and the bad of it, the sweet and the bitter. I do not shed tears over it. I did not choose my lot, but though circumstances shaped and directed it I wrought the ending of it at least with my very own hands.

When I spoke to my fellow slaves of freedom and revolt I was daring the gods to bring on this day. When I planned and schemed and thought out every step, I had been looking into the eyes of this gloomy hour. When I struck my master's head and crushed his skull I had sealed my doom.

I did not ask to be a slave. And my hands wished and yearned for tools to work the earth that belonged to my people, for clay with which to make things of beauty and of use, for weapons to poise not against humans but animals, in order to feed and clothe myself and those around me.

They yearned as they do still for Vallida's gentle beauty, and I look at them now with strange emotion and wonderment. These are the hands that had cut their chains, and then they killed a man. In the last hours of life, it is said, a man makes a reckoning with his conscience for the deeds he has done.

And so I look upon myself and feel no sorrow and no shame. I did what had to be done It may be that other men will hear of our deed. It may fire their hopes, give strength to their arms. Perhaps some of my brother slaves have gained their freedom, though mine was shortlived indeed.

As for my conquerors, I fear them not.

I shall walk with head held high amidst the jeering throng.

And when they shout "Glory to the Roman Empire!" I shall whisper with my last breath "Death to the Roman Empire! Our time is not far from coming."

Here come my jailers.

Farewell.

To Santa Claus, Farewell

"How I wish for snow," sighed Andy, his little face plastered to the window pane.

"Mommy, isn't it true that Santa Claus cannot come unless there's snow?"

For weeks preceding Christmas, Andy, who is six, has been rendering me helpless with just such questions.

"Can anybody live on the North Pole?" he would say innocently.

"No, I'm sure not," I would answer, confident of the logic of my statement.

"Well, Santa Claus does," he would say triumphantly, and I would flee the room in disastrous retreat.

You see, Andy, who is a highly advanced little boy, fervently believes in Santa Claus. He can read books about dinosaurs intended for fourth graders, add several three-digit numbers in his head faster than I can, and study a foreign language as seriously as any adult and with more success. But in his heart of hearts he is an incurable romantic. Even when he was a little tyke, his acquiescent applause to Peter Pan's question: "Do you believe in fairies?" was the most enthusiastic one you heard.

The idea of Santa Claus was first introduced to him when he was slightly over two years old by—God help us—his parents, and he was immediately enchanted with it. No one was more excited than our Andy about the presents mysteriously deposited by the mythical Santa. With all his heart and soul he threw himself into the spirit of the thing.

We, on the other hand, were so thrilled with his unbridled happiness and never ceasing wonderment over the seeming miracle that we played it for all it was worth. Andy's older brother, who had lost illusions ages before, tolerantly participated in our deception.

I remember shuddering even then at ever having to shatter Andy's innocent, childish delusion. I knew that the moment of reckoning would come some day, and I could only hope that we'd manage not to have it happen too soon.

"How will we ever tell him it's merely a story?" I would say to my husband.

It was now mid-December, but the weather had been unusually mild. Then at last it turned cold quite suddenly, and all of Andy's hopes materialized.

Snow, rich and full, had fallen overnight, covering the garden, trees, and shrubs with an immaculate, shimmering whiteness.

Andy's brother was in bed with a cold, and Andy enthusiastically volunteered to help his father shovel off a pathway to the street. He came back as vibrant as he had been when he first undertook the arduous task. Cheeks red, high brown boots filled to the brim with snow, hands wet and frozen under the fur mittens, he announced with pride:

"Dad could never have finished the job without me!"

Later he came to me carrying a book about children of other lands, which he said he had just "discovered" on his bookshelf. The book had belonged to his older brother, and I had transferred it to Andy's room only recently, thinking that perhaps he would be ready for it some time in the future.

"It says here," he said excitedly, "that you don't have to pack a suitcase and take a ship or plane to go to other countries. All you have to do is read the book and you're there!"

He thrust the book into my hands.

"Read it, Mom. That's exactly what it says."

I resisted the impulse to tell him that I was busy, didn't have time to look at his book, and that I believed him. I glanced at the short preface. I looked at his shining, eager little face.

My little boy was growing up.

An hour or so afterwards, as I was in the living room dusting the piano, he came in again.

"You know, Mom" he said very seriously, "Robert said he does not believe in Santa Claus."

Robert is a year older and, therefore, somewhat of an authority. He's our neighbor and Andy's best friend.

My hand holding the dust cloth froze in midair. Andy continued, unabashed.

"Well, I believe in Santa Claus."

Then he paused reflectively and added:

"There are a lot of kids who don't. Aren't they silly, Mom? Of course there's a Santa Claus, isn't there?"

The moment had finally come. It was as obvious as the little frown on Andy's forehead that if I acquiesced in his childish dream at this point, he would find only too soon that I had told him a lie.

But I lacked the courage, and I fled to the kitchen where my husband was writing a term paper for a graduate course he was taking, with books and pamphlets strewn all over the kitchen table.

"He wants me to confirm the fact that there is a Santa Claus," I gasped. "He just asked me point blank, and he says that Robert doesn't believe in Santa."

My husband rose to the occasion with all the courage I lacked.

"Well then," he said, "it's time to tell him the truth. Right now."

"But it's almost Christmas, how can we?" I protested.

Andy sauntered into the kitchen. "I know what you're saying," he announced accusingly.

"What?" we replied in unison.

"You said there's no point in having a Christmas tree because there isn't any Santa Claus. But you can't fool me."

"Andy, that is not at all what we said," replied my husband.

"Andy, dear"—somehow a particle of courage had come to me.

"Once, long ago, in a European country lived a good, kind old man who was rich and loved children. Many children in his land were poor and could not have any toys, even at Christmas time. This man would buy many toys, load them into a large bag, and leave them at the doorsteps of the poor children. In the morning the children would find their presents, and there would be great rejoicing. The name of the kind man was Nicholas, and his legend grew. Ever since then, to honor him, we surprise little children with toys on Christmas morning."

Andy, who had slipped into a chair while I was speaking, sat in shocked silence for a long while.

"Last year I got presents," he finally said. He was afraid to ask the precise question of where they had come from.

"They were from us," his father said. "You see, Andy, parents tell children about Santa Claus because they want them to be happy." He went on, trying to penetrate the cloud of sadness that seemed to envelop the little boy and to take away some of his pain.

"When you are a little boy it is wonderful to believe in Santa Claus, but we feel that we should tell you the truth now that you are growing up. A lot of children already know that there really isn't a Santa Claus, and you might argue with them that we told you there is. It's the spirit of giving that really counts, anyway. Parents give their children gifts because they love them."

Andy hardly ever cries. Most of them time he displays self-control astounding at his age.

But now his chin began shaking ever so little, and tears trembled in his voice just below the surface.

"How then," he said, pulling out his last trump, "how do all those presents get under the tree?"

"We put them there," answered my husband. We were both looking at Andy, and our hearts sank. He did not quite want to believe us yet, but the arrow had found its mark. He was upset, he was hurt. *We* had hurt him.

Perhaps I could still arrest the cruel process, I thought, and I looked imploringly at my husband. Maybe we could postpone it until next year? As if he were reading my thoughts he said:

"Someone is bound to disillusion him before long."

Then he turned to Andy and said:

"But you know, Andy, you still have a Santa Claus."

"Where?"

"Right here!" his father exclaimed, pointing to himself.

We all laughed. The awful tension of the preceding moments was broken, and the glistening tears receded from our child's eyes.

"When I was in college," his father went on, "I dressed up once in a Santa Claus suit, with a big pillow stuffed in front to give me a fat belly. Then I went into a kindergarten class and said 'Ho! Ho! Ho! Who has been a good little girl or boy this year?'"

And Andy, who is blessed with a good sense of humor, laughed heartily at this image of his father.

"Those kindergarten children all believed I was the real Santa Claus," his father continued. "Can you imagine that?"

They laughed again, together now in their superior knowledge, at the poor, deluded kindergarten children.

When Andy went upstairs to his soldiers and his blocks, I continued to sit at the table, contemplating the past half hour.

Had we, inadvertently, in our parental honesty and wisdom, wiped some of the magic from the world of make-believe for our child? Did we shut a door that could never again be opened? Had we done the right thing?

I did not realize that I had said the last sentence out loud.

My husband answered, "It was awful and I hated to do it. But I think it was the right thing."

When Andy came bouncing down to supper several hours later, he did not look the least bit shattered. He was full of enthusiasm for his new Civil War game, and instead of eating, proceeded to compose a letter to his grandparents.

Later that evening he reminded my husband of a rash promise to take him sleigh riding.

"It's fifteen degrees outside," his father protested. "However, if you really want to," he added, weakening.

Andy really wanted to.

As his father took the sled down from the attic, Andy remarked:

"When you brought the sled home last year you said it was because it was too heavy for Santa Claus to carry. Now I know why you said that."

And he smiled at his father, and ran happily after him into the snowlit night.

Only I, the mother, was left behind to regret the passing of my little boy's childish, beautiful illusion.

"To Santa Claus, Farewell" draws heavily on an experience with our younger son, Andy, and was published in the collection The Invisible Passage *in 1969.*

Papa's Tea

Papa liked his tea strong and piping hot. He would come into the kitchen, his dignified, fastidious figure in utter contrast to the disorder that reigned all over the room. With a helpless glance at the large kitchen table on which, as usual, lay an infinite variety of objects of non-culinary character, he would ask:

"Well, where is Mama? I'd like some tea."

Where was Mama? Where was the wind, he could just as well have asked. She had flown off an hour, maybe two hours ago, no one knew precisely when. Where was she off to? The bakery maybe, or the dry goods store? She was going to look at that piece of blue wool for my sister Bessie's new coat, so maybe that's where she went.

"Max, where did Mama go?"

"I don't know," came a disgruntled reply from my brother. "Don't bother me."

"Oh, for a glass of tea," sighed my father. "One glass, what am I saying? I could drink a dozen glasses."

What was the matter with Mama? She never could remember the time Papa was due home. Even if she did, she was sure to find some errand that couldn't wait, and forget all about him.

Not that there was anything personal she had against Papa. Oh, no. Didn't she often forget when we were supposed to come home from school for a quick half-hour lunch, and didn't we end up crying in the street dozens of times until some neighbor would feel sorry for us and let us in? And when we would berate her afterwards, she would say:

"I know, I know. I only went shopping for a short while. So why couldn't you wait five minutes?"

That was Mama. You couldn't change her and you couldn't make her understand certain simple facts of life, I thought, as I went into the kitchen, determined to take care of Papa. One just had to accept Mama as she was. And she was wonderful in so many ways! When she sang near the open window, it was as if all the sound and glory of a spring morning in the country had found its way into our Bronx apartment. The neighbors would hang their heads out of the windows to listen and comment:

"Mrs. Siegel, how you can sing! Like a regular opera star."

And Mama was always smiling. Sometimes there really wasn't anything to be cheerful about, but Mama invariably found some little

thing to make her happy. Maybe it was a concert in the park, or a ticket
to the opera, or the neighbor's fat new baby, or the pretty dress she had
just made for me with her beautiful, clear stitches. I often wondered
how a person so untidy in her household chores could sew so perfectly
and be so painstakingly neat in this work. And she never, never hit us.

Her mind was always on beautiful things. And how she loved
pretty clothes! Next to music, I guess she loved clothes just about the
best. When the tailor got through making her a handsome new suit,
Mama would go out and buy a twenty-dollar silk blouse to wear with
it.

We all thought she looked simply stunning. She was a little thing
with a lovely head of brown hair, and elfish face, and a good figure,
despite her lack of height. She carried her clothes well. But what
happened to these clothes when she took them off!

Papa was fond of saying:

"Mama needs nice clothes so she can keep them under the kitchen
sink."

And he wasn't far from wrong. Her things were everywhere except
in the closet where they should have been. Once she got it into her
head that she wanted a mink stole. Papa only said:

"Mama wants a mink stole so she can keep it underneath the wash-
tub." And that was the end of that.

In the kitchen, I put my arms around Papa's neck.

"How is my Lily today?" he said, and smiled in that special way he
reserved only for me. Even though there were four of us children,
Papa's preference for me was acknowledged by the whole family and
resented most by my brother Max.

"Papa's darling," he would jeer at me when he got good and mad.

"Go in the living room, Papa," I said. "I'll make you some tea."

"Thank you, Lily dear, that would be very nice," Papa answered,
and he walked out.

The kitchen table was a real mess! There was the fabric for my skirt,
and the pieces for Bessie's new hat, and two pots from last night's
supper, and seven dirty spoons and forks, and the cookie jar, and the
pot of jam from breakfast, and last Sunday's paper! The disarray was
not exactly out of the ordinary. Only the items changed from time to
time. Even when Mama happened to be home, the table was so piled
up with bundles that there was barely enough room for a plate or two.

I put the two pots in the sink, and began removing the other things one by one. For once Papa would have a completely clear table to drink his tea!

I found a pretty plate with rose clusters to put under the glass, and a white napkin. Where was there a clean spoon? I got the kettle going and prepared the tea. I took Mama's bundle of fabrics to her bedroom, the "dump" room. This was where we hastily dumped everything that lay all week long on chairs and couches and the floor when a visitor was announced. Why did the house always have to be so disorderly? It would look exactly the same when we came back from school as when we had left in the morning.

"But Mama, I'm ashamed to even bring a friend home," I would complain.

"If you don't like it, stay home and do it yourself. I got too many other things to do."

"But you know I have to go to school, Mama."

"So, is that my fault?"

What could you say?

The kettle was whistling. I ran back to the kitchen. What was that Papa had said?

"I could drink a dozen glasses." That was it!

He shall have a dozen glasses then! My heart was bursting with love for Papa, who was so good and kind. I knew how determined he was that we, his children, should have a better life than he himself had led, and how hard he labored to make it come true.

Papa's father was an innkeeper in a Russian town. His first wife, Papa's mother, came from a wealthy family and stayed with him just long enough to bear him two sons. Then she divorced him and married the town mayor. My grandfather promptly married a widow with two little girls. One of those girls was Mama! Grandfather was of sturdy stock, and proceeded to outlive this wife of his, and then married twice more, each time outliving his much younger wives. Finally there were seventeen children in the house, and Papa, as the oldest, bore most of the responsibility for them. Mama was a very determined person even when she was little. As Papa told it:

"When we were children, Mama decided that we would get married some day. As far as I was concerned, I could have stayed single all of my life!"

Mama had a good voice and wanted to go on the stage, but instead was apprenticed to a dressmaker. Still, she managed to sneak out every now and then and sing in cabarets, until her stepfather would find out and drag her home virtually by the hair. But did this stop her? No. At the very next opportunity she was out, like a spark of flame, dancing, singing, enjoying herself. Life beckoned to Mama with irresistible force.

Papa felt responsible for her even then—for her, and the whole brood of children, until he was drafted into the czar's army. This was a calamity, and Mama was in despair. She saved money from her earnings as a seamstress, and it was arranged, over Papa's protests, to have him smuggled over the border the first time he came home on leave. Mama took care of getting him a passport and a change of clothes, bribing whomever was necessary, but Papa resisted to the very last. It wasn't legal, he said. It was not the proper way of doing things, and Papa was a very proper person. Well, they got him over the border somehow and then onto a boat bound for England, where an uncle lived.

There Papa, who wanted to be an artist, became a house painter so that he could earn a living. As soon as he had mastered the trade he was shipped off to America with a letter of recommendation to a "lantzman" on the Lower East Side of Manhattan. He worked and saved, and sent for Mama. She too moved into a "lantzman's" railroad flat, and went to work sewing in a factory.

They didn't get married right away. How could they afford it, with so many brothers and sisters back home to send for? First, there was Aunt Esther. As soon as she came she fell in love with a cousin, and the foursome worked to bring more relatives to America. Next came my Aunt Minnie. But that was after Mama and Papa got married and moved uptown to a five-room apartment. Aunt Esther and Uncle Abe moved in with them, and when Minnie came, naturally she moved in too.

Papa said to Minnie:

"Now it's your turn to go to work and send for your sisters."

But my Aunt Minnie wasn't that altruistic. Besides, she hated to work.

"I should work for them?" she said. "To hell with that!" Aunt Minnie didn't mince words.

"But Minnie, how can you behave like that?" Papa asked. "Didn't we send for you?"

"So what!" was her answer. "I don't feel like it."

"Well, if that's the case, then maybe we'll let your sisters stay back in the old country," said Papa.

Aunt Minnie finally went to work for about a year, but hated it so much that as soon as Uncle Sam proposed to her she married him, although she was only sixteen and he was over twenty-five. From that moment on, she wiped her hands of her family in Russia. It took years for Papa to save enough money to try to bring more of them over, what with his own growing family to support.

By that time it was very difficult to locate them. They were scattered all over what was now the Soviet Union, and had families and roots of their own. Besides, the government made it impossible for them to leave the country. Papa never saw them again.

I was rummaging in Mama's cupboard, trying to find twelve clean glasses. Then I tiptoed to the living room to steal a look at what Papa was doing. I didn't want him to discover my surprise a moment too soon!

Papa was sitting with his dictionary and a pad, writing down his daily quota of words. Papa read a lot, mostly Jewish books and Jewish newspapers. But he also made it a point to study Webster's dictionary, increasing his vocabulary by at least three words each day. He would write the definitions painstakingly on a little pad, and never forget them.

"Why aren't you a businessman like Uncle Hymie, Papa?" I remember asking him once. Uncle Hymie lived in Brooklyn and had a fancy car.

"You really are so clever, Papa. You could make a lot of money, I'm sure!"

"Because, Lily darling, I'm just not made to be a businessman. A businessman, he has to be a little bit crooked. Don't let anybody tell you it isn't so. You can't make money in business being a hundred per cent honest. But your uncle Hymie, he is made to be a businessman. Even when we were children together in Russia, I knew he would be a businessman one day."

"Why, Papa?"

"Well, I'll tell you. On Saturdays when our father would go to shul, your uncle Hymie would set up a little business of his own. There was a window at the inn that opened out onto a side street. And under this window was a high, long table. Your uncle Hymie would have a show right under that window, on top of that table, and he would charge money for it. A kopeck apiece to all the children in our town, and they could see the show from the outside. And business was good! Sometimes he would make a whole ruble on a Saturday!"

"But how, Papa?"

"Well, he would just pull down his pants and show his behind to the other children for a kopeck, that's how!"

"No, Papa!" I collapsed, convulsed with laughter.

"So you see, Lily, that's how I knew he would be a businessman," Papa concluded triumphantly.

Here were the glasses at last. I counted an even dozen. Some of them didn't look any too clean, so I took them down from the shelf and reached under the sink for soap. I pulled out Mama's skirt instead, the one with the front pleat. She had only had it a month! Oh, well, the soap must be around somewhere. There was Bessie's slipper that she'd been looking for all week! Here was the soap, finally. I washed the glasses with care, making them shine for Papa. Where could Mama be all this time? I bet she went to the movies. There was a new musical at the Prospect, that's where she must be! Mama and her movies!

I smiled at the memory of all the movies she and we had seen together. We the children, I mean. You see, Papa works very hard, and during the week he likes to be in bed early. Nine o'clock and he is snoring away. But not Mama. Night does things to her. Her eyes begin to shine, her little feet begin to dance with impatience. She must be off and going somewhere. Sometimes I think that only with the advent of night does Mama begin to realize fully her fierce joy of living. And it is not until the early hours of the morning that she begins to lose her nocturnal sparkle, and makes ready to surrender herself to death-simulating sleep.

Well, the four of us children have to be put to bed. That is, four of us since a year and a half ago, when Claire was born. Until then there was just Max, Bessie, and I. Papa needs his rest, and Mama must go out to see a movie. Since we children make a lot of noise all alone by ourselves, Mama worked out a perfect compromise. She'd take us along.

As soon as Papa was asleep, Mama would dress us all—including Claire, the baby—and off we would go to the movies. We would settle ourselves as comfortably as we could, for we were good for the night. Mama had to see the picture several times over, and often we would not go home until the movie house shut down for the night. Mama watched the movie, and we slept until it was time to go home. She even got these nightly excursions down to a science. We would be wearing our pajamas underneath our clothes so that we could jump right into bed when we got home. Mama would open the door as quietly as she could, and warn us as we staggered into bed:

"Shh! Don't wake Papa!"

It was nearly three years before Papa caught on to the fact that his whole family was missing, night after night. At that point, Claire had been going with us for over a year. It seems that Papa had an attack of indigestion, and got up at about 11 P.M., looked for Mama, then took a peek into our rooms. Nobody home. Well!

When we tiptoed in that night, who should be sitting in the kitchen but Papa! What a rumpus there was! I have never seen Papa so mad. He took a plate and broke it right before our eyes! We all hid, but we could hear his roaring.

"The children have to go to school! What do you mean by keeping them out so late? And a baby, too!"

He went on like this, fuming and shouting for quite a long time. Mama just sat there.

Finally she said, calm as calm could be:

"You're finished?"

"Yes, I'm finished!" Papa roared.

"What do you expect me to do? I'm not going to stay home night after night. If you want, I'll leave them home."

And that's just what she did. From then on there were no more nightly escapades. All went well until one night when Claire had a fit. She demanded Mama's presence, and Papa couldn't calm her down. Finally, exasperated and worn to a frazzle, he gave her a good spanking. The next day, sheepishly, he said to Mama:

"From now on, you take *her* along." So Claire was the only one of us children qualified to be a movie critic.

I had the gleaming glasses neatly arranged on the table. An even dozen! I brought over the sugar bowl, a little lemon. That's how Papa liked it. The tea smelled delicious. I poured it carefully, and didn't spill a drop.

"Papa, your tea is ready!" I called.

As he came into the kitchen, I pointed proudly.

"A dozen glasses, just like you wanted."

Papa looked surprised.

"But Lily, darling, I didn't really mean . . . ."

He reached for his eyeglasses, and wiped them with his handkerchief. Then he took me around and began to laugh. It was a happy kind of laughter, and I was relieved, because for a moment I thought he was going to cry. I guess he was pleased with his tea. But instead of drinking it, Papa kept laughing and laughing. I don't remember when I had heard Papa laugh like that before.

My, it was good to hear Papa laugh!

"Papa's Tea" was originally published in The Invisible Passage *collection in 1969. It is decidedly not autobiographical, but rather is based on some experiences told to me by my friend Jean Baker. It was reprinted in 1980 in* The Woman Who Lost Her Names, *the first collection of stories by American Jewish women writers, and in 1987 in* Family: Stories from the Interior.

Hello, Grace?

Grace stood before the medicine chest in the bathroom and examined her face critically in the mirror. Was that thin crease directly beneath each lower eyelash one of the telltale signs of approaching middle age? The stray gray hair among the brown, the ever so slight puffiness of cheek, were as plain and undeniable as the relentless onward march of life. Grace sighed. There was not much one could do to halt the cruel process, except to regret youth's passing She had always felt a hundred years old anyway. Now she was on the way to looking it as well. In a few short years she would be forty.

Thank goodness Gene likes me anyhow, she consoled herself as she crossed the hallway toward the unmade queen-size bed in their bedroom. Involuntarily she smiled, thinking of her husband's still handsome, lean frame, and the blackness and thickness of his curly hair. He, at least, had not changed much. Neither had the steady, strength-giving power of his affection.

"I may as well make the beds," she thought, shaking off her momentary depression. "The kids will be home for lunch before long, and I haven't done a thing but brood about myself all morning."

The kids. The sweetness and fullness of her feeling for them overpowered her for a moment. Hers and Gene's two boys. The salt of the earth, the hope and pride and the promise for the future.

Insistent ringing of the telephone broke the circle of her contemplation.

"Hello, Grace? This is Alice. Surprised?"

"Sure I'm surprised. How have you been?"

"Fine, fine. How long is it since I've spoken to you? Two, three years?"

"It must be almost three years," answered Grace, once more musing on the swift passage of time.

She had gone into Manhattan to do some department store shopping—one of her rare trips into the city from suburbia—and had dinner with Alice in a 57th Street restaurant. Gene was away and her aunt was with the children, so after dinner she went with Alice to her room in a midtown residence hotel for women.

She could picture it clearly as Alice was speaking—the narrow cubicle with the washed-out scatter rug, the virginal-looking bed, the small table with a dirty cup and saucer and some half eaten cakes sent up by room service. She now imagined Alice sprawled out on that bed, her long blond hair falling dangerously over her mouth and eyes, the receiver in her limp hand.

"Well," Alice drawled, "even though we haven't seen each other in a long while, I thought you'd be interested. I'm engaged."

"How wonderful!" Grace's enthusiasm was genuine and her sigh of relief almost audible to the other woman. "To whom? Not Richard, I hope."

"Oh, not that Greek! That's all over with for a long time. I gave him enough years to make up his mind, don't you think? No, it's someone I met a few months ago."

"I'm really glad for you," Grace repeated. "What is he like?"

"Well, I'll tell you in the strictest confidence. He comes from one of the finest, oldest, and wealthiest families. His father is an investment banker and president of all kinds of boards and charities, they have an estate in Maryland, a very well known family. They're related to —— and the ——." Here followed a list of names, impressive enough to stagger anyone.

"That sounds great, Alice," Grace said slowly, as the enormity of Alice's news sank in.

"But you know me, Grace. I would never, ever go for anyone just because he had money, you know that, don't you?"

"Sure, I know, Alice."

"Well, he's simply gorgeous, that's all. Six feet two, the most handsome boy you ever saw. I'm crazy about him, just crazy about him. You know I'd have to be mad about him to want to marry him, don't you?"

"Yes, Alice, I know," she again consoled her. Still there was something not quite right with the picture. Why would a fellow with all those advantages want to marry Alice? Alice at twenty-two had been bad enough, but Alice at thirty-nine? In that hotel room, three years earlier, observing with a slight pang of pity her friend's lonely existence, she had asked:

"How old do the girls in this place think you are?"

Alice shrugged her shoulders, making her long, somewhat unruly hair swish about as she spoke.

"Oh, they all think I'm about twenty-four."

"It's fantastic," Grace later told Gene. "Alice still lives precisely the kind of life she did when we were in college. Nothing has changed for her except the name of the hotel. The presence of all those young kids doesn't make her the least bit uncomfortable. She simply pretends that she is still one of them."

"How old is the fellow you're marrying?" she now asked Alice.

"Oh, he's thirty-three."

"Does he know how old you are?"

"Well, I told him I'm thirty. You know I don't even look *that* old."

"But how can you keep up such a pretense? He's bound to find out sooner or later, and what will he think of you? Besides, I don't see why you can't tell him the truth."

"Don't worry, he won't find out. By the way, did I tell you his name? Hal. Isn't it romantic?"

"Tell me, Alice, has he ever been married before? How did such a desirable fellow escape this long?"

"He used to be a pretty wild boy in college—you know, love affairs with all kinds of girls. He tells me all about it, every detail. It just simply kills me, every time he does it. We meet a girl in a restaurant, and later he'll tell me he's had an affair with her. I get insanely jealous, as you can imagine. No, he was never married before. He was with the army in the Normandy invasion and suffered some kind of shock. He spent a long time in hospitals afterwards recuperating, and didn't have time to get involved."

"I see. Is he all right now?"

"Oh, yes. He still sees a psychiatrist regularly, but he's all right. And I've been very good for him. He's terribly in love with me and I love him like I've never loved anybody in my whole life. I think it was just fate that we met, don't you? That I didn't marry Richard, I mean, and that Hal was sick all that time and didn't fall in love with another girl. It was meant to be, that's all. His mother and sister are coming in from Washington this weekend to meet me."

"How is *your* mother, Alice?"

"Oh, fine. She's just thrilled about all this. You know she gave up all hope of my getting married."

"Well, I'm glad for her too. That's a big worry off her mind."

Alice's Mother. Grace's soft heart ached again for Alice's mother.

Grace had met Alice through Laurette, who had the room next to hers at the Cosmopolitan House, a home for foreign and American students of both sexes. Laurette was as close to a roommate as one could come to in Cosmopolitan House, where all rooms were singles and the two genders, male and female, were carefully separated in different wings.

One day Grace found a fascinating creature reclining on her friend's bed. Dressed in skin-tight sweater and skirt that showed her spectacular figure to ample advantage, long blond hair in streaks of light and dark, falling into her eyes, deathly pale makeup, and a garishly oranged, puckered up mouth, she stretched her long fingers with carefully tended, blood-red nails toward a box of candy.

"Grace, I'd like you to meet Alice. We went to high school together."

"Hi, Grace," Alice said easily.

She smiled, and Alice noticed her protruding front teeth, large and ugly. There was a smear of lipstick on her upper teeth.

Conversation around Alice consisted of two subjects, mix them as you will: Alice or men, Alice and men, men, Alice. Grace was amazed at how knowledgeable Alice seemed about men. By comparison she felt naive, inexperienced, if not downright stupid. Alice appeared to have been born knowing what men were all about. Her appearance was contrived to entice men and to invite passes from them. Yet her exterior covered a prudish and ice-cold heart.

Although Alice was game enough to lead the gullible creatures on, she was never willing, so to speak, to let nature take its course, and would indeed drive men to utter distraction. Then she would complain:

"What's the matter with me? I can always get one date, but they never take me out again. What have I done?"

"It's what you haven't done, my dear," Laurette would reply. "And after having promised so much!"

"What do you mean?" Alice would begin defensively, but never quite finish.

The day Grace met her for the first time, Alice suggested that they all go down to the Cosmopolitan snack shop, for that is where one could meet men. Grace had a paper to write, and Laurette said she wanted to rinse out some underthings, so Alice went alone.

"Well, what do you think of *her?*" Laurette asked as the door closed after Alice. Grace, hypnotized by the image of the suggestively wiggling behind that had just disappeared into the hallway, shook herself awake to say:

"She's quite something, isn't she?"

"She sure is." Laurette evidently did not approve.

"What did she come here for? To visit with you?"

"No, don't be silly. She comes here to hunt. Very few eligible men left in Westchester nowadays."

Alice came a great many times after that. When Laurette was not available she would camp in Grace's room, for Grace had never learned the art of being rude. She would invariably find her dresser cluttered with an array of cosmetics—powder spilled all over the books—stockings, shoes, and undergarments scattered all over the chairs and bed. Alice did her hunting in the lobby and in the coffee shop, and she was remarkably successful. It's true that she was not always very choosy, but she invariably wound up with a date. Often Grace or Laurette would arrange to have a cot put into one of their rooms (a custom at the House), and leave the door open so Alice could slip in late and spend the night.

Once Laurette, in a surge of bitterness, told Grace about Alice's background. Her mother had been a child bride. She had married a rather wealthy older man, and it proved to be a most unhappy union. There was a divorce, and Alice went to live with her grandmother. (Alice's father lost all his money in the stock market crash, and she never saw him after that.) The grandmother had spoiled her scandalously, until one day she died of a heart attack. Laurette very dramatically claimed that "Everyone knows Alice killed her grandmother."

Alice's mother, who had remarried in the meantime, took the child to live with her. Her husband was a widower with a little girl of his own, a lovely quiet youngster. Alice burst into this household like a fury, disrupting everything, capricious and demanding, doing her level best to break up the marriage. She was idle, she was rude, she was always lounging around, she did not go to school, she had no desire to go to work. Her stepfather despised her, but her mother was forever defending her only child. Finally, Alice's mother took a job "just to take care of Alice's refined needs," Laurette said. Alice's clothes always came from Saks Fifth Avenue, and she was forever paying tuition for extension courses at the university, which she never finished, for this was merely another device to meet men. Once this purpose was accomplished, finishing the course became unnecessary. Besides, Alice had no stick-to-it-iveness. When Grace met her, Alice was already a twenty-two-year-old drifter who had never done a stitch of work in her life. Her mother was forty-three, and working to keep her little darling satisfied.

Not long after Grace and Gene were married they had found a furnished apartment in a small private house in Westchester. When they had been settled in their newly acquired abode for several weeks, Grace realized that they were only a few blocks away from Alice's home. She called Alice, who urged Grace to visit her as soon as she could.

While Grace covered the few blocks that separated her from Alice's home, she recalled what Laurette had told her about Alice and her mother, before Grace was married.

"And for all that sacrifice, she treats her mother horribly. You should hear how she speaks to her. Mark my words, she will be the death of her one day."

The apartment building was a respectable, middle-class structure; the lobby was light and spacious. Grace took the elevator three flights up, and rang the doorbell. Alice opened the door.

She led Grace into a wide hallway, opening onto a dining area, beyond which she could see the kitchen on the left, on the right a large bedroom, and the living room toward the middle. From the kitchen came a pleasant, trim-looking, brown-haired woman.

"How nice to meet you, Grace," she said in a soft, subdued voice. I like her smile, Grace thought. Somehow she had never pictured Alice's mother quite like that. Instead, she had imagined a brassy, tall blond, with a booming voice and aggressive manner, someone more in step with Alice.

"I have heard a lot about you," Alice's mother continued. "And I know you've been a good friend to my girl."

"Look here, Mom, she didn't come to visit you. She came here to see me, so stay out of this," Alice demanded imperiously. Grace, taken aback, smiled with embarrassment at Alice's mother as Alice propelled her toward her own bedroom.

After an hour or so of listening to Alice's confessions (Alice had a way of interminably repeating herself, frequently interspersed with "you know what I mean"—but her self-preoccupation was so unconscious that she was almost amusing), her mother interrupted them with:

"Coffee and cake, girls."

The dinette table was beautifully set, with a gleaming white tablecloth and napkins, white cups, a bowl of fruit, and a plate of cake.

"God damn you," Alice said, quite calmly and matter-of-factly to her mother. "How many times do I have to tell you that I hate that cake?"

In a loud aside to Grace:

"She'll never learn, that stupid woman!"

Grace sat in shocked and embarrassed silence.

Alice's mother seemed to take no notice whatever of her daughter's crude remarks.

She poured the coffee.

"One or two sugars?" she asked Grace.

"One, please," Grace answered. Sugar had only recently become less scarce now that the war was over, and it was still a new experience to be offered such a choice.

Alice's mother sat down.

"Why the hell don't you have your coffee in the kitchen? Must you butt in here?" Alice said. Grace, no longer surprised, became angry.

"Won't you sit with us, Mrs. Highland?" she said quietly but firmly.

Alice's mother, with a quick glance at her daughter, sat down.

"I worry so about her," she slowly said. "I wish she would meet a nice boy and get married. You know how things are around here. It's not the easiest thing for her or for anyone else."

Her glance swept the apartment. Grace thought of the husband who couldn't abide Alice.

"Always trying to shove me out of here, isn't she? I'm still young, what the hell is my hurry," Alice said.

"Not that she is not welcome here," her mother continued gently. "This will always be her home; she's my child, after all. It's just that I want her to be happy."

The cry of all mothers who mean well. Alice's mother had meant well. She cooked and cleaned for her, and bought her clothes, and took her abuse, and made of her a parasite, a leech, a creature who preyed upon others, forever unable to face up to the joys, the responsibilities, and the pain of life. Yes, Alice's mother had meant well.

At thirty-nine, Alice, who consented to work only intermittently, was still in principle supported by her mother. Fortunately her stepfather had made a great deal of money, and her mother no longer worked. Instead, she stole from her food allowance and sent money to Alice surreptitiously, for she did not dare tell her husband that Alice had persisted in her lazy ways. This arrangement was facilitated by the fact that Alice lived in a Manhattan hotel, and was supposedly holding a job downtown.

The memory of all this flashed through Grace's mind with the quickness of a dream, between Alice's last sentence on the phone and her next.

"We're going to Europe on our honeymoon," Alice was saying. "And Hal says we might buy a house in Scarsdale, though can you imagine me not living in town? I'll have a maid, of course, so I won't have to do any housework."

"Well, Alice," said Grace lightly. "It's obvious there is no justice in this world. You've always been a lazy bum, and you're gong to stay a lazy bum for the rest of your life. Good luck to you."

Alice laughed happily and launched into a long and involved description of her future husband, his family connections, her breakup with Richard, who had been her lover for seven years (it had taken her three years to finally make up her mind to have a true love affair with him in the first place), her, Alice's true love for Hal, (again, "it's not the money, you understand"). Grace's ear began to hurt. The unmade bed stared at her accusingly.

"Look, Alice," she finally said. "I'd love to hear some more but I really have to get going on my housework. I'm thrilled about your engagement and you both have my best wishes. Why don't you two come out and have dinner with us? You've never even seen my children."

"You know I never travel out to Long Island," Alice replied.

"Call me, then," Grace said. "Maybe when I come in to do some shopping you'll introduce me to your beloved. Anyway, send me an invitation to the wedding. I'll even buy a new dress in your honor."

"Oh, we don't plan any elaborate affair. Just the immediate family."

"Let me know when it happens then. And call me when you get a chance. Okay?"

She hung up before Alice could get started again.

Grace tidied up her room first, then crossed the hall to her older son's bedroom. Would Mark ever learn to be neat? She bent down to pick up a dirty pair of socks from the middle of his blue rug. His sneakers peeked at her from under the dresser, and a pair of dusty dungarees lay over a brand new white shirt that must have fallen out of the closet as he was hastily dressing. The bed looked as though a pair of baby elephants had wrestled on it. As she picked up the sneakers she looked at Mark's sports trophies standing on his dresser—one for basketball, two for football. He was all boy, and, with Gene's teaching, growing into a fine human being with a feeling for fair play and decency.

She walked over to the window that looked out into her large, pleasant garden. Yellow and orange marigolds winked up at her. If I hustle through this job I might go out to do a little weeding, she promised herself. A redbellied robin preened himself on the fence. I will hurry, she decided.

They had been lucky to get this old colonial house at a price they could afford. Everyone said they had done wonders with it. Still, it hadn't been easy, and sometimes Grace longed for a few frills that she knew could so embellish life.

Speaking of frills, she thought again of Alice for whom life would now be one frill after another. She had never really liked Alice, she freely admitted to herself. But she was grateful for her and her forward ways—she had been for years. For had Alice not gone down to the lobby of the Cosmopolitan House to hunt one Saturday afternoon, Grace would never have had Gene, and she did not even wish to imagine what life might have been without him.

She remembered the day well. Alice had come from Westchester as usual, had parked her little satchel in Grace's room and gone down to the lobby. After an hour or so she came up again.

"I have a date with Eugene for tonight," she announced.

"Eugene?" Grace repeated with amazement.

"Yes, I just talked to him for half an hour."

"What about?"

"Philosophy. He's very intelligent."

Grace had just reached the opposite conclusion about Eugene. If he and Alice could discuss philosophy, then the boy was obviously a congenital idiot!

Eugene was new to Cosmopolitan House. He had moved in only a few weeks before, and Grace had noticed him at once. Such a tall, straight, and handsome American was a rarity during the war. She wondered what had kept him out of the army. Only later was she to learn of the knee injury he suffered while playing varsity ball.

She had been peremptorily introduced to him among several other new arrivals, but she was not sure he even noticed her. Since he did not say hello to her afterwards, she shyly ignored him.

Alice, however, was not shy. Alice had a date with Eugene after a half hour's conversation.

The following morning Alice, as was her habit, filled Grace in on the most intimate details of her previous night's date.

Gene had been lucky, as Grace liked to tell him later, that he did not get fresh with Alice that night, or she would have had something to hold over his head for the rest of his life.

"He took me dancing," Alice told her. "To a very nice place in New Jersey. But he's a funny boy. Afterwards he parked the car and I talked. He just sat and listened—never even made a pass at me."

Grace, for some reason, felt relieved.

"Not that I care," Alice continued. "You know I'm crazy about Richard, and if we didn't have a fight I'd be going out with him instead."

They went to the dining room for breakfast. After breakfast, Alice wanted to sit in the lobby.

"Richard might be coming down, and I don't want to miss him," she said. "Please sit with me, so it doesn't look too obvious."

Grace, resigned, went and got the Sunday *Times* and settled down in an armchair.

"There's Eugene!" cried Alice. "Hi, Eugene."

Eugene came over and was once more introduced to Grace. Alice wandered away for a moment. Eugene asked if he could have part of the newspaper. Grace handed it to him silently.

She didn't know how, but a few minutes later she found herself embroiled in a hot argument with him. He had made some cynical statement about the war in Europe and its probable outcome.

"This war will change nothing," he stated. "We're supposedly fighting for democracy, but for most people the world will be the same miserable place after we get through."

"If I believed that," Grace said icily and quite self-righteously, "I would commit suicide right now. This may be nothing but a cliche to you, but there will be a bright new world when this war is over."

"You're kidding yourself, my dear girl," he repeated, a trifle patronizingly.

Grace got up. "What a rude boy," she thought.

Aloud she said: "Will you please tell Alice that I've gone up?"

"Sure."

She attempted a dignified exit.

Five minutes after she got to her room her phone rang.

"Hello, Grace, it's Alice. How about going to Van Cortlandt Park with me and Eugene? Pedro will come as your date."

"No, thanks," said Grace. Pedro was a good-looking but empty-headed Brazilian who was always eyeing Alice's curves rather hungrily, and Grace did not like him.

"But Eugene has a car," Alice tempted.

Grace had always had a weakness for cars. And a car with gasoline in that day and age was a rarity, what with war restrictions and rationing. She weakened.

"All right, I'll be right down."

All the way to the park Alice, who sat in the front seat next to Eugene, kept leaning over him seductively. She was urging him to teach her how to drive. Pedro was trying to get affectionate with Grace in the back seat, but she gave him such a dirty look that he froze in mid gesture. Eugene kept up an easy banter. He seemed relaxed now, and

Grace was surprised to find him quite witty. He was making unmerciful fun of Alice, but she could not help laughing because he was so clever about it. His victim did not even come close to catching on.

Later on, Grace, stretched out in the boat on the lake, looking at the sky, caught Eugene watching her. They bought frankfurters at a park stand, sat on the grass, and began talking about books and serious matters. Alice and Pedro, bored, walked away.

They had dinner at a restaurant near the Cosmopolitan House, and Grace strolled back to the House with Alice and Eugene. It was easy walking with him, it seemed to Grace, and she almost envied Alice her date.

"You kids want to be alone," she said as they reached the lobby.

"Not at all," protested Eugene, but Grace, who thought he was being polite, went upstairs.

There was a knock on her door a few minutes later.

"Alice? What are you doing here?"

"I got tired of listening to him talk about you. He thinks you're the most wonderful, interesting, and loveliest girl he ever met. You've got it made, kid."

She had. It was Eugene from then on—always Eugene, with his easy quick wit and his generous, sensitive heart. She had a lot for which to be grateful to Alice.

She was still in the garden when the kids came home for lunch. She heard the banging of the screen door, sounds of racing footsteps. Drew sounded unhappy.

"You weren't fair," he was saying tearfully to Mark. "You didn't give me a head start, and you pushed me!"

"Listen, you little squirt, I gave you all the breaks and still you couldn't win. I'm faster than you, what do you expect? Is lunch ready, Mom?"

"I'm sorry, dear, I completely lost track of time. I just have to wash my hands. Take some juice in the meantime."

She stole a quick look at Drew whose mouth was trembling suspiciously.

"Darling, you can't always win, you'd better get used to that. That's life. And Mark is much bigger and older than you! As for you, my young man," she addressed herself to her older son, "how many times have I asked you not to call your brother names?"

Two minutes later they were sitting at the kitchen table, eating sandwiches—Drew with his perpetual baloney (baloney was his middle name, according to Mark) and Mark with his tuna fish, their passionate argument totally forgotten.

"Do you think I'll be able to play in the Little League next year, Mark?" Drew was inquiring.

"You won't be old enough even though you're good. You know, Mom, he's really better than kids two years older than him, I'm not kidding."

"Yes, I know," she replied. "But he will have to learn that he can't rush the years away. There is plenty of time."

He *was* good, that little Drew with his bright, shining face under the mop of blond hair. Good at everything. His quick mind would think nothing of tackling involved mathematical problems way beyond his years, or books several levels above his grade. He was all confidence, breathless enthusiasm, and desire to know and experience the world around him. And in his small body resided side by side, Grace knew, quiet courage and a boundless capacity for love. Sometimes in the enormity of her love for him she trembled for this son of hers even more than for the other. If anything ever happened to him! Yet she knew that she must struggle against the desire to over-protect him. The secret of constructive love, she had read in some book or other, was to hold with an open hand.

The subject of her musing was addressing her now:

"Mom, I promised Billy that I would go over to his house this afternoon. May I?"

"Yes, Drew, but be back in time for supper."

"Susan wanted me to go to her house instead but I explained that I promised Billy. I told her not to be sad. I said that I feel lonely sometimes and I go to my room and read or play with something."

Mark, reading the sports section of the *New York Times*—at least he reads the *Times*, Gene would defend him before Grace—did not stir.

"Come on, Drew, you've got to go back to school. You're always such a slowpoke when it comes to eating," Grace said.

Mark suddenly came to life and threw down his newspaper.

"So, you're not going over to Susan's today, lover-boy?" Instantly Drew was up in arms.

"I'm going to get you for this!" But Mark was already halfway out the front door. All Grace heard was the sound of his laughter and hurried footsteps on the path to the street. Drew took after him like lightning.

"Boys!" Grace cried in warning, only half expecting to be heard.

She turned to the breakfast and lunch dishes as soon as silence again fell upon the house. The skin on her hands was growing rough, especially around the right index finger and her nails. She was forever breaking them as she scrubbed sinks and floors and planted her garden. She bet Alice's hands would never look like that. What was the matter with her that she couldn't get her mind off Alice!

Well, she may as well face the truth. She was a little envious of her friend's outrageous good fortune. That stupid Alice, who never read a book in her life, never had a serious thought in her head, would forever be spared the greasy domestic chores that sapped her, Grace's, vitality and deprived her of the energy and time for creative endeavor. Her unfulfilled ambition to be a writer flooded Grace with renewed bitterness. When? When in the maze of her daily cleaning, washing, mending, child-tending hours would she find the time to write the stories and books, the ideas for which spun crazily in her head when she could not fall asleep at night? She was thirty-seven now, putting it off until she could afford some help, putting it off, she knew, probably for good.

Grace, who suddenly felt very tired, climbed the steps to the second floor. She took the vacuum cleaner out of the closet. There were suspicious looking swirls of white dust around the scatter rugs in the upstairs hall and bedrooms. She wished they could afford carpeting. It would be such a time and energy saver. This too would have to wait. Gene was now a college professor, an assistant professor to be sure, and his salary could not quite provide wall-to-wall carpeting. But he loved his job, and that was important. Still, wouldn't it have been nice if Gene's family were rich and illustrious like Alice's fiance's, instead of down-at-the-heels farmers? What was it Sean O'Casey had said? "Money isn't everything but it sure saves a lot of wear and tear on the nerves." A honeymoon in Europe, indeed. It would take a minor miracle for her and Gene to take a trip to Mexico within the next ten years.

That evening she told Gene about Alice's call, but he didn't seem very impressed. Weeks passed and she did not hear from Alice. No wedding announcement came in the mail. Soon she forgot about it. Three months later, searching through her address book for the phone number of a washing machine repairman, she came across the address to which Alice had told her she was moving, that of a swanky apartment hotel on the East side of Manhattan.

"Gee, I wonder what happened to Alice?" she said to Gene that night. "Did she get married I wonder?"

Gene took his eyes off *The Collected Works of Karl Menninger*.

"That fellow's parents probably took one look at Alice and hustled him off to a mental institution," he said.

Undaunted by her husband's sarcasm and feeling a little guilty about her own lack of interest, Grace dialed Alice's number the following day.

"Miss Highland's apartment, please," she said when the switchboard operator answered.

"Just a minute, I'll see if she's answering her phone today," was the reply. Alice was getting mighty important, Grace thought.

In another moment she heard Alice's usual lazy drawl:

"Hello, who is this?"

"It's Grace. How have you been? You seem pretty hard to get hold of."

"Oh, I've been so busy that I've been leaving a message downstairs not to let anyone disturb me. I'm always running around with Hal."

"How is he?"

"Oh, fine, fine. We're planning to get married in the spring." Then in a whisper, "He's always around. I hardly even have time to wash my hair."

"How did you like his parents and they you? Any problems?"

"No, his parents are just crazy about me. They're very pleased that we're going to get married and they think I've been a very good influence on Hal. His mother is very good looking, young looking, you know, and very social. But to tell you the truth, it's getting a little on my nerves, his hanging around me all the time. I haven't a moment's privacy."

"Doesn't he work?"

"No, he's got all sorts of trust funds and investments, and he doesn't have to work."

"But isn't he planning to do something? It's no good for a man to have no occupation. Even if he's rich he could surely find something to interest him . . . ."

"No, he doesn't want to," Alice said categorically. "He's not interested in anything. Just in watching me, all the time. He's so jealous he even wants me to dye my hair a darker color so I won't attract attention from other men. I've only a half hour now to fix myself up a little, while he's sleeping."

All this was said in a tone so dejected that Grace became slightly alarmed.

"I still think Hal should have something to occupy him," she suggested lightly. "It would be good for both of you. Can't you think of anything he might do?"

"No, there's no use. He doesn't want to work."

After Grace hung up, she was troubled. Not that there was anything tangibly amiss, yet the entire setup made her a trifle uneasy. Alice had sounded discouraged, defeated, weary. It seemed to Grace that some shapeless, indefinable trouble lay in store for her.

"I must be imagining things," she finally persuaded herself. Perhaps a touch of her own unresolved envy had made her seek imperfections in the glittering fabric of Alice's future. Perhaps.

Months went by and Alice did not call, did not send a wedding announcement. Life sallied forth in all its complexity, days like beads, strung on top of other days, some brighter, some darker in hue. Drew had a bad attack of croup, and Mark's football team failed to win the championship. Gene decided to finish his doctorate and was working late into the night. Snow fell and covered the garden, and birds foraged for crumbs that Grace set out for them beneath a large fir tree.

One December morning Grace woke up with a nasty headache. As a result, she was sharp with the boys and short with Eugene. It was a relief when they all left, and she could drink her cup of coffee alone, in a quiet house. She loved the winter stillness that so insulated her from the world outside. She had never been as gregarious as Gene, preferring solitude and books to the sound of human voices. It was a failing, she knew, and she tried to meet his need to see the people he liked and enjoyed, at least from time to time. Coffee always dispelled her headaches and bad moods, and she was regretting her early morning grumpiness.

The phone rang. It was Alice

"Hello, Grace?. I thought I'd let you know I got married a few weeks ago."

"Congratulations, kid! How wonderful!"

Alice did not reply for a moment. Then she said:

"But my husband doesn't love me, Grace."

"Don't be silly. What are you saying?"

"He's lying on the bed, pretending to be asleep. But really he doesn't love me."

"Is he listening to this?"

Alice is losing her mind, Grace thought. Then as if speaking to a mental patient, she added consolingly:

"I'm sure you're just being foolish, Alice. I'm coming into town tomorrow to get some shoes. Why don't you and Hal have lunch with me?"

"No, I don't think so. We don't see anybody." A pause. Then:

"I'm sorry I can't talk to you. My husband wants me to get off the phone." Click.

Grace, puzzled, replaced the receiver slowly. Even for Alice this was a little peculiar.

At around six that evening, as she was preparing dinner, with the boys banging a ball in the room directly above the kitchen and giving her another headache, Alice called again.

"Hello, Grace? I'm alone now," she said. "And I have to talk fast. That monster will be back any minute. He might even be listening at the door right now. Just a moment, let me check."

She went away for a few seconds.

"It's okay," she announced.

"Grace, you have no idea what I've been through. It's unbelievable, that's what it is. Unbelievable. I'm going out of my mind."

"Alice, get hold of yourself," Grace said, thoroughly alarmed. "What's wrong?"

"I'm a prisoner, that's what. I have to stay with him and take care of him in a one-room apartment every minute of the day. And he beats me, Grace, he hits me really hard."

"What are you talking about?"

"He's sick, he's a very sick boy, Grace. I told you he'd suffered an awful shock during the Normandy invasion, didn't I? Well, that isn't the half of it."

Alice paused, as if unable to go on. Grace, worried and compassionate, asked gently:

"Alice, what are you trying to tell me?"

"He's a drug addict, has been ever since then. Barbiturates. In and out of hospitals. Several times he nearly died from an overdose but can't live without it. When he's on the stuff he's unpredictable, even vicious."

"But, Alice, didn't you know this when you married him?"

"Sure, I knew. And like a fool I thought I could cure him. I talked with his psychiatrist the other day. He said: 'This boy has had the finest medical care money could buy. And if we couldn't help him in fifteen years, then how did you expect to?' You know, Grace, he can be almost human in the evening, then he'll wake up in the morning and start hitting me as hard as he can. 'Who are you?' he says to me, all of a sudden, can you imagine that? I left him once already, you know. I went to my mother."

"What did you tell her?"

"I told her I had a little argument with Hal. So she said I should go home and make up with him. I can't tell her the story. In the meantime, I gave up my apartment, and all my things are here in Hal's room."

"Aren't you going to move to a larger place?"

"No, he doesn't want to do anything except take his drugs and sleep. I've got a charge account in every department store in town and I can't even go out to buy a dress. All that money and we don't touch a penny of it, except for drugs. Once in a while he suddenly goes out like he just did. Then he takes all the money out of my purse so I can't run away again."

"Alice, isn't there anyone you can talk to, anyone who can help you? You told me his parents were very nice; can't you speak to them? Don't they know what's going on?"

"They know he's sick, but they don't guess the half of it. I can't tell them. And none of my friends in town will let me stay with them either because they're afraid of Hal. He can be pretty frightening and dangerous, believe me."

"Look, Alice," Grace said, thinking quickly. "You've obviously got yourself into a nasty mess and you must extricate yourself from it. Leave him. You can find a job, and until you do, try prevailing on him or his parents to help you financially. He's a wealthy man."

"How can I leave?" wailed Alice. "What about all my clothes? And the jewelry his mother gave me? You don't know him, he wouldn't let me take anything out of here. I'd have nothing to put on my back, and it would take me ages to replace everything. I just don't know what to do. Sometimes he tells me to get the heck out but he doesn't really mean it. He even wants me to have a baby just so I'll be tied to him for good. Shhh, I think I hear him."

Silence for a long, tense moment. Alice was back on the phone, saying in a completely altered voice:

"Have you heard anything from Laurette? I understand she had another baby. My sister saw her mother the other day and she said the baby was adorable."

Hal had returned.

Grace was badly shaken by Alice's revelations. She kept worrying about her, expecting hourly to see some dreadful item about Alice spread on the pages of a sensation seeking newspaper. She pitied her friend, the waste of her husband's life, and she pitied his family.

According to Alice, Hal had once been a popular, promising, and seemingly well adjusted college boy. What hidden tortures of the soul had been unearthed in him, what terrible guilts had been bared by the cruel scalpel of the surgeon called war? The psychiatrists had despaired of the cure. And his parents? She understood their anguish. The black sheep of an illustrious family, with all the money in the world proving insufficient to wipe away the stain.

"I must do something to help her," she said to Gene. "I can't just sit by—he might kill her or something."

"Look, honey," he answered. "Calm down. She walked into it with her eyes wide open, didn't she? You know this couldn't have happened to a normal person. You can't help her. No one can."

And so once more, though with greater effort this time, Grace put Alice out of her mind.

Months later she received another frantic phone call, made from a phone booth in the lobby of Alice's hotel. The time was eleven thirty at night.

"How can I get to your house, Grace? Can I take a taxi?"

Grace gave her directions.

"Have you enough money, Alice? A taxi all the way out here from Manhattan will be very expensive, provided you can get a cab driver to want to come out this far. Why don't you take the subway and then a taxi from the station to our house instead?"

"Don't be silly. I haven't been on the subway in ten years. I've got my makeup case with me, that's all. Hal threw me out just now, so I decided to really take him up on it. It's raining, isn't it? Maybe I shouldn't come out tonight, then. I may not be able to get a taxi this late anyhow. Well, I guess I'll go back up. Maybe I'll come tomorrow."

"Alice, how is everything?"

"The same, no change. He didn't really mean it, you know. He just told me to get the heck out of there, so I went. I'll see you tomorrow or maybe some other time. So long, Grace."

Grace walked away from the telephone. She knew with sudden clarity that Alice would not leave the unhappy, tortured man on that or any other night. In a way, Hal was no more than she deserved, for hadn't Alice long ago also turned her back on the realities of life? In their own peculiar, sick way, they were really quite suited to one another.

Grace went upstairs. She was too absorbed to notice the slightly worn spot in the brown stair carpet which, inherited from the former owners of the house, never before failed to annoy her. Drew was breathing regularly, his favorite pillow in the shape of a star propped up next to his head, a book about rock collecting spread half-open on the table next to his bed. Mark, as usual, was sprawled all over the bed in a wildly awkward position. Automatically she bent down to pick up a pair of dirty socks from the floor. As she threw them in the bathroom hamper she heard Gene's door key turning in the downstairs lock. He had a late class. She ran down to him, and impulsively threw her arms around his neck.

"Hey, what's this?" he said, pretending surprise, but she knew he was pleased. His rough cheek felt cold as she kissed it.

"Hello, Grace?" was published in the collection The Invisible Passage, *1969. It's partly autobiographical and is also based on a person I knew. Some time after its completion, Alice's (the names have been changed) drug-addicted husband took a fatal overdose when she managed to get away from him. Although he was very wealthy he left her penniless, but his family gave her a gift of one million dollars—because she had his name.*

History's Choice

General Alexandrov seldom drank. But now he walked over to the round, brown table covered by a large white doily on which his mother-in-law, Elizaveta Popovna, had set out a bottle of vodka and several glasses. He refilled his glass and raised it in a silent toast to a woman's photograph placed on the closed lid of an old baby grand piano.

This was, after all, an occasion. He wished he could share it with his wife, doctor Natasha Alexandrova, who died heroically at Stalingrad, and who had left behind her an empty place in his life.

The comrade from the Politburo had barely left. There had been little time for the enormity of the news to sink in.

The comrade was an old friend. Even so, his greeting had been particularly effusive. He kissed the general on both cheeks and banged him several times on the shoulder, all the while laughing heartily.

"Alexandrov! Alexandrov! What news! What congratulations are in order!"

The general, puzzled, answered the embrace from habit rather than jubilation. He wasn't due for a promotion. Did his daughter Irina, on tour with the Bolshoi, score a particular triumph in the coveted role of Giselle? Or did his son Alexei, with the Red Army in North Vietnam, advance to the colonelship to which he so aspired? Still, this would not have called for congratulations from so high a source. The general waited for his friend to go on. Patient waiting had been so much a part of his existence that he sometimes thought he had been born merely to endure it all of his days.

"It's Vassily, your son Vassily, you old so and so!" roared the comrade from the Politburo.

"Vassily?" the general repeated, unbelieving. This second son of his, the most beloved and closest to his heart, had always been singularly lacking in ambition. He was on a mission with the Air Force, and the general had not seen him for six months.

"Yes! Your son Vassily, the first man to orbit the globe in a spaceship! Alexandrov, your name will live in glory forever in Soviet history! We have shown the capitalists up! We've done it!"

The general raised the glass with his second drink to his lips. He downed the liquid in one quick gulp. In the kitchen Elizaveta Popovna was coughing, something she did only when unable to contain her excitement and pleasure.

What was it the comrade from the Politburo then said?

"We've sent him up and we've brought him down. It's not official yet, but I thought it would do no harm for you to know now. We'll announce it in a day or so and then we will laugh in the face of the world. Let us drink to that, Alexandrov! You have a very famous son."

Foreign and local news correspondents had been kept waiting since Friday on a twenty-four hour alert. Momentous news was to be announced, and speculation ran high. It was pretty well understood that the expected announcement would concern a man-shot into space. Rumor had it that Lieutenant Vassily Alexandrov, the son of a famous Red Army general, had successfully completed his assignment as the world's first astronaut. Doctors were still examining him, and various scientific data were being coordinated. Washington had already unofficially admitted defeat. The newsmen, cursing the delay, waited.

Captain Sergei Babin was fast asleep, though troubled by dreams. Even when he closed his eyes, it seemed as if the interminable routine of tests continued. A future astronaut was supposed to have nerves of steel. Well, his were giving out, and before long they were sure to notice.

Someone was shaking him vigorously. Sergei awoke with a start to see his immediate superior and another man, a civilian with light blue, piercing eyes, standing by his bed. He was asked to dress at once. Sergei glanced at his watch. It was one thirty a.m. How old was he? Twenty-four, yet he knew his lessons well—never to question, never to inquire.

Darkness enveloped him as he stepped out of doors to where two men were waiting. A car took them to the airstrip. Barley fifteen minutes later they were way up, above the clouds.

Lights burn late in the Kremlin. And so they did, as was their custom, on the night Captain Sergei Babin was led inside and met the Big Man.

Shining beads of perspiration stood on the Big Man's bald pate, and several already empty whiskey bottles were on his huge desk. But if anyone, including Sergei, thought the Big Man did not have a firm grip on things, he was sadly mistaken.

"Captain Babin," said the Big Man slowly, as his foxy little eyes quickly scanned the tall figure of the airman. "Sit down!"

Then to one of his aides, who hovered anxiously near him:

"Give him a drink."

"Well, then, Captain Babin," the Big Man addressed him. "We have brought you all the way here to tell you about a big promotion for you. In fact, we are going to promote you right into outer space!"

The Big Man roared, and his explosive laughter evoked a similar response from his associates.

"Your comrade Vassily Alexandrov has, it is true, preceded you in that respect. Nevertheless, since he isn't feeling quite up to par, you are going to take his place in history. What do you say, Babin?"

Sergei sat in stunned silence, only half understanding what was wanted of him.

"Come on, say something, you fool! You don't mean to let your country down, do you? We are going to make you immortal! Do you understand? In six hours we will announce your successful completion of a journey into space. Kolagin here," he pointed to one of the men, "will brief you on all the details. Remember—no slip-ups!"

Dismissed, Sergei rose and automatically saluted the Big Man. It was all clear now.

"I shall do my best, Comrade Chairman," he said. In his ears rang the distant roar of cheering crowds.

Tuesday morning General Alexandrov awoke to the heavy pounding in his temples. Somewhere Elizaveta Popovna was shuffling about in her house slippers. What day was it? He switched on the radio. Wasn't it just about time for an announcement about Vassily?

It was several minutes past the hour of the news broadcast. The announcer was speaking in an excited voice about another glorious achievement of the Soviet Union that proved decisively the superiority of the communist over the capitalist system.

"Our first cosmonaut is a simple peasant's son. Yet he has soared to the loftiest heights and gained a place forever in human history. Only under socialism was such a supreme achievement possible . . . ."

A peasant's son? The general's head was spinning.

"Sergei Ivanovich Babin," droned on the announcer, "our first cosmonaut, a true son of the people . . . ."

The words crashed through the general's skull.

"Vassily? What have they done with Vassily?"

Moscow had never been in a more festive mood. From the Big Man to the lowest street cleaner the people celebrated and rejoiced. The news spread across the length and breadth of the Soviet Union and reverberated all over the planet. Soviet man reigned supreme in the conquest of space. The entire world bowed in awe and admiration, and sent congratulations and the highest of praise.

The city waited for the triumphant arrival of the first "cosmonaut," Sergei Babin, from whatever spot on the Soviet map the scientific knowledge of the country's best brains had returned him.

It was the silence of his colleagues when he encountered them in the corridors or offices of the Defense Department that was even more terrible to General Alexandrov than all the rejoicing and the shouting outside.

Silence had formed an invisible wall all around him. No word had come from the comrade in the Politburo; no word, in fact, from anyone.

The general sat at his desk for a long time, staring at the wall, his lips, despite all his willpower, forming the silent question:

"My son. What has happened to my son?"

He saw Vassily as the fat, healthy infant he had been, dangling again on Natasha's knee, grinning from ear to ear. "Smiling Vassily" they always called him, the child who had never caused them even a moment of pain.

By afternoon he could endure it no longer. He closed the door and fled from his office.

On his way down, he passed the open door of a large meeting room. Several newspapermen were standing about, talking to Kostia Nikitin, the information officer.

"Come on, Kostia," the correspondent of *Le Monde* was saying in his passable Russian. "Nobody wants to tell us anything. How did he land? Parachutes?"

"Gentlemen, the pilot was in his cabin. The descent was successful. That is all we can say for the present."

At the street entrance the general nearly collided with the departing newsmen. An American correspondent was scarcely an arm's length from him. The general slowed imperceptibly, prompted by an inner trembling.

What if he were to speak out?

Irina? Alexei? Was he to sign their death warrants? And to make his country a laughingstock before the whole world? The trembling passed; the general quickened his step.

At the Metropole Bar AP was talking to Reuters. AP said:

"I can't help thinking there is something not quite kosher with the whole picture, you know what I mean? That premature report in the London Daily Worker, that long wait, and even some of that cosmonaut's statements, like looking out and seeing the earth in a band of blue . . . then we're told by one of their own scientists that the capsule had no windows . . . ."

Reuters, reaching for his drink, said:

"Relax, old boy. It's hit us all pretty hard, you Americans most of all. It isn't exactly pleasant to have the Russians beat you to the punch again. Accept the bitter truth. They're ahead of us in space exploration, so smile, and congratulate them, even if it hurts."

"I guess you're right," AP replied, and ordered a double whiskey soda.

The general decided to walk the short distance home. The clear, cool air might be good for his aching head.

On his right he passed a pretty park that had always been one of his favorite spots. He went in. He could cut across it, save several blocks, and have a breath of fresh air besides. It was still too early for the leaves, but patches of grass were beginning to peer valiantly through the covering of melting snow.

Was that the rustling of last year's leaves underfoot, or was he already being followed?

He turned his head ever so slightly to one side—there was no one behind him. General Alexandrov walked alone with his fear.

Enormous, faceless, it was to be with him from now on. How long did he have? A week, a day, an hour?

His key turned heavily in the lock of his apartment door. All was still inside. Elizaveta Popovna must be out doing the marketing.

The general took off his coat and went into the room where his wife's picture stood on the piano. He picked it up.

"Something terrible has happened to our Vassily, Natasha, and there is nothing, *nothing,* I can do about it."

His son Vassily was gone, without a trace or a word of recognition, vanished as though he had never existed. The general was too old to have any illusions on the subject. Had not his old friend, General Petrov, disappeared after his return from Republican Spain?

A car door slammed and steps resounded on the pavement below. He went over to the window. A black Ziv limousine was parked across the street. Two men in light-colored raincoats were walking slowly, methodically toward the building.

Was it just his imagination, or did their eyes for a split second scan the windows of his apartment? So it was to be now, he thought.

He put down the photograph.

"History's Choice" was first published in the collection The Invisible Passage *in 1969, and depicts my disillusionment with the Soviet Union and the communist idea. It was based on some news reports at the time, but it is entirely fiction.*

One Summer

My mother's cousin Elaine did not live in our town. She taught school somewhere in the provinces. I usually saw her during summer vacations, but sometimes during the winter recess as well. Even then she did not spend much time with us. She liked to stay a few weeks with her parents and her sister Bea, and she would then be off on a train "to see the country."

Cousin Bea, a studious looking woman of thirty-five, was hopelessly nearsighted, but would only wear glasses in public when she absolutely had to. Exceptionally brilliant as a student, she became one of the first woman architects in our country—we lived in Central Europe—and now worked in my father's office as his assistant. Her mother, my Aunt Esther, desperately wanted cousin Bea to marry, but cousin Bea was very choosy. All sorts of wonderful matches were proposed to her, and Aunt Esther saw to it that many supposedly casual meetings with eligible men were arranged, but cousin Bea turned up her nose at all of them.

Cousin Elaine, who was much younger than cousin Bea, was very pretty, so no one yet worried about her getting married. But people were saying that it was getting kind of late for the other sister, and if she didn't make up her mind fairly soon she would wind up an old maid.

My father's office was on the ground floor of the modern structure that he had designed and in which we lived. The trend toward that kind of forward-looking architecture was gaining momentum in Europe. My father was fast becoming a famous man in his field.

In the morning before breakfast, when he was still shaving, or right after the dinner hour—we ate dinner in accordance with the European midday custom—cousin Bea would appear with documents, blueprints, lists of forgotten or important appointments. My father said she was a very efficient and conscientious nag. Despite the quality of lightheartedness about him, one felt instinctively that he was the sort of man who took serious things seriously and did not let small matters have an overbearing effect on his mood. He could be relied upon to do a marvelously creative job when he was really interested. The more challenging and difficult the job, the more interested he became.

Cousin Bea, on the other hand, worried about everything. Therein existed a true spiritual kinship between her and my mother. They even resembled one another physically. I can still picture them, like two plump, bespectacled owls huddled over the dining room table set for afternoon tea, lost against the hugeness of the antique furniture, commiserating with each other on the vicissitudes of life. Invariably they both gravitated toward that one room, whose heavy mahogany, intricate silver, and cut crystal had been inherited by my mother from her parents. It represented the last stronghold of tradition in our ultramodern household.

I had early discovered that my mother was primarily, or even exclusively, occupied with herself. This was just as well as far as I was concerned. In principle I resented her lack of warmth and interest—mothers were supposed to be concerned with their daughters' welfare according to society's rules—but I really did not like her as a person. Her own behavior merely served to exonerate my guilt.

As soon as the front door closed after my mother I would gratefully retreat into the deliciously scented haven of Anna's kitchen. Anna had a triangular sort of face, framed by heavy braids that coiled around her head. She had a husband, a strapping fellow who was out of work and who used to visit her only on Sundays. She was no ordinary cook. She had traveled out of the country and was very worldly, I thought, not at all like the other village girls who had worked for us before she came.

It was a wonder how she handled the heavy work that was hers from morning to night, and her hands were coarse from washing dishes and scrubbing floors. Technically we were supposed to have a girl in to help her, but my mother would usually pick a quarrel with the new servant, or simply dismiss her for some imagined incompetence, and Anna would end up doing all the chores.

My constant dread was that she too would leave us one day. But my mother never argued with Anna. Instead, she would beat a hasty retreat from the battlefield, go shopping or to one of her several charitable institutions, to play bridge or to meet her friends at a favorite cafe. Once I went to the orphanage of which she was a devoted patroness. The girls there told me enviously that I was lucky to have such a mother. She was very nice to them and they thought her simply wonderful. Of course, they were orphans and I wasn't, I reasoned, so she didn't have to be nice to me.

My father had been a very "handsome boy," or so everyone said, and through the years, although he had lost much of his wavy, romantic-looking hair, he continued to cut a dashing figure. On short visits to summer resorts, which he made with me but without my mother, all sorts of ladies would buttonhole me privately to say:

"That isn't *really* your father? He must be your older brother!"

Sometimes I half wished he would look his age, but I was secretly proud that he appeared so young, so vibrantly alive.

I had been made to understand by various relatives on my mother's side that my father's people stood much lower on the social scale than my mother's, who were a prominent family in our town. I thought fiercely that a grave error had been committed somewhere. It was my debonair father, with his well-cut clothes and fine hands who was the aristocrat, not my fast aging, overweight, not terribly intelligent mother.

My mother's parents had once had a great deal of money, but had lost it all through foolish investments before she was married, so if my father had been searching for something it certainly could not have been money. Whatever it was, it had evaporated long since. Tradition, convention, and the mores of the town made them stay together, living as comparative strangers in the same household. Yet every so often my mother would explode and my father would then turn as calm and cold as marble. I understood even then that it was useless to try rekindling feelings long dead, but she never gave up and kept stirring up the ashes, making an occasional spark fly. I hated the explosions even more than the usual undercurrent of quiet unhappiness that flowed through the house. They served only to intensify my private uneasiness at having a different existence from the normal stream of life.

It is said that childhood is a time when we're most carefree and untouched by the stresses of the adult world. Never believe it! Childhood is constructed of inner torment, the most awful of doubts, and of loneliness, made more bitter by one's ignorance of the vast brotherhood of universal despair.

There were always women in my father's life. First they emerged as mere shadows, snatches of overheard conversation. He attracted them like a magnet, and with things as they were at home he was naturally not averse to their attentions. But his affection was fickle, never lasting. It was to be so all of his life. To his loss, the only female to whom he was able to remain steadfast was myself.

Once when I returned a copy of *The Magic Mountain* to a shelf in his private office and was leafing through my beloved *Forsyte Saga,* a small snapshot fell out of a brown envelope stuffed into one of the books. It was a picture of my father on shipboard—in summer he always traveled to faraway places. On a chair next to his, turning ever so slightly toward him with adoring eyes, sat a stunning blonde. He was smiling up at her. The whole thing gave me quite a start. It was one thing to hear about his love affairs but quite another to see visible proof. I did not begrudge him his romantic escapades, but I wished he would not leave his pictures around. That destroyed the illusion I had carefully built up that in my home all was as it should be. I put the photograph back in the envelope and the envelope somewhere in the bookcase. I'd be careful not to find it again.

One summer during my adolescence my father decided to stay home instead of taking his usual foreign journey. I abhorred his absences; I felt hopelessly lonely. His decision added warmth to the thought of a long rest from the deadly routine of school.

The weather was mild. Cousin Elaine came into town early in July after a week in the mountains. The strawberries in the garden were late. Someone jumped over the wire fence and mutilated our best yellow tea rose as soon as it had bloomed. But even the pain of that wanton destruction was assuaged by Father's presence. He was invariably cheerful, and my ears grew accustomed to the sound of his jaunty steps. My best friend, Adrienne, and I had reached a quiet understanding in those few weeks when the pressure of school had eased. It would be hundreds and hundreds of precious hours before I'd have to face our mathematics teacher again. Life was truly good.

Then Father grew restless. He began talking of Italy and the Alps, and the peace of summer was broken. He finally settled on a famous spa within the borders of our own country, packed his elegant luggage, and was gone, barely getting to the train on time, as was his custom.

Just before he left he told me:

"I want you to promise to join me if I find suitable accommodations. I'll write in a few days."

At any other time I would have jumped at the chance of going with him, but that summer I wanted to stay home. I wanted to be quiet and alone with my own books and mementos, in my own room, and to talk to Adrienne, to read and dream a little. But I said:

"All right. I'll come when you send for me."

Father was unable to find accommodations in the famous spa, but located a lovely hotel in a smaller resort close by.

"Of course this would not be as gay for you as what we originally had in mind," he said in a letter, "but perhaps you could persuade cousin Elaine to come along with you for company." Cousin Elaine was agreeable enough, and within a week we were on our way.

The resort was perched on a small, square plateau, surrounded by fir-covered mountains. Its several stolid hotels faced this geometrical figure on two sides. The third was taken up by a large modern structure, the last word in European luxury hotels, where we stayed. The square was banked with flowers and dotted with benches, trees, and shrubs. In a strategic spot squatted a white concrete shell beneath which an orchestra played every afternoon from two to five. All was subdued, aristocratic, graceful, and incredibly boring. A restful quiet reigned over the lushly green mountainside. One saw other people only at long intervals, and even then they seemed lost amidst the flowers.

Neither Father nor cousin Elaine seemed to mind the deadly quiet and isolation of the place. In fact, they both seemed to thrive on it, taking long walks in the woods and admiring the scenery. Father maddeningly whipped out his camera on every conceivable occasion. Picture taking was something I rarely endured, feeling all the more awkward next to cousin Elaine's womanly and attractive figure. Her ash blond hair fell in gentle waves around her lovely face. My own hair, brown and straggly, hated from the very bottom of my heart, made, I was sure, an awful contrast with hers. Next to my pale skin, cousin Elaine's pink cheeks bloomed with even greater health and vitality.

She was always in excellent humor, and the sound of her laughter permeated those days. Only once did a frown crease her forehead, quite unnecessarily I thought. It was when she noticed the hostess in the hotel restaurant making eyes at Father, and indignantly called her "that stupid girl!"

It was silly to get upset about things like that, I thought. Women were *always* flirting with Father.

I greeted the end of that vacation with unbridled relief. Several weeks still separated me from the inevitable return to the monstrosities of Latin grammar and the labyrinths of plane geometry.

"Aren't you pleased we're leaving this dreadfully dull place?" I asked cousin Elaine on the train. Cousin Elaine, whose pink cheeks seemed a little paler than usual, nodded vigorously.

"Oh yes, it's time we were going home."

Ten days later, when I returned from my friend Adrienne's, our house wore the unmistakable air of having undergone one of its periodic explosions. Anna's face was strangely set, and I bumped into cousin Bea, scurrying from the scene of disaster. Did the door slam in my father's office downstairs?

My mother lay on the chaise lounge in her bedroom. A white handkerchief had been dramatically flung on the floor, and I saw at once that she had been crying.

"What's wrong?" I asked, to be polite, though I did not particularly want to know.

She turned a tear-stained, bitterly twisted face toward me and hissed:

"Your father and cousin Elaine have been carrying on a love affair behind our backs all summer!"

Involuntarily I lifted a hand to my face, which stung as if from a slap. In her fury my mother paid no attention to the effect her words were having on me.

"I found a letter in the pocket of his bathrobe—from her. It makes everything crystal clear. It's a perfect scandal!"

She began to sob.

I backed out of the room, slowly, in stunned, helpless silence. The blow was almost more than I could bear.

It had taken but an instant to realize that my adored father had used me as a pawn in his love affair, and the knowledge hit me like a ton of bricks. It was a betrayal of confidence so enormous as to be almost unforgivable.

My sympathies were not with my mother. She had no emotional claims on my father; theirs was nothing more than a business arrangement—it had been so for years. I despised her for reading a letter not intended for her eyes. If anything, I loathed her even more for telling me about it.

But my father's conduct in relation to myself? That was quite another matter.

All the details of my pleading with Elaine to join us—at his urging—and of our strange vacation together suddenly fell into place. How could I have been so naively stupid! And how could he have allowed himself such an indiscreet involvement! This was no distant love affair of which nothing but a picture remained, but a scandal right within our own family, in the town in which we were known and respected. It could leave permanent scars.

For the first time in my life I was angry at my father, with the most terrible, self-righteous anger of the very innocent and very young.

Despite my fears the "scandal," which boiled for days, stayed within the strict limits of our household. My mother issued ultimatums, demanding the end of the romance or she "would spread the story all over town." Cousin Bea was instructed to carry this message to cousin Elaine, but she demurred. She would not, she said, interfere in her sister's private life.

Anna, all-wise in the kitchen, perceived that I was in on the secret, and grumbled:

"Your mother's cousin Bea is in love with your father herself. She has been all these years. Why do you think she refuses to get married?"

Was there no end to shocks?

I retreated into a hard, outwardly unfeeling shell. Only Father never acknowledged the existence of a crisis—certainly not when I was in his presence. I did not speak about it to him; how could I? I ceased speaking to him altogether in those awful days. My anger was full and my wounds festered. The gall of his betrayal stood between us and choked down my words.

Summer hobbled to a close. The "scandal" gasped and then slowly died. Mother did not move out as she had threatened to, and cousin Elaine left town. Father made no move to follow her.

What did they say to each other when they met for the last time? I've often wondered, but I was then too unforgiving to care.

Then cousin Bea said casually to me one day:

"I wish you would make it up with him. He's impossible at the office."

Remorse touched my pain-hardened heart. Its sister, pity, was not far behind. I had to face it. I was fourteen, and my father was not a god. He was a man, subject to a man's passions and mistakes. Did one episode of insensitivity to my feelings cancel all the years of his devotion? It was cruel to go on punishing him. Hadn't he stayed with my mother for my sake since I was knee-high? What did I know of the emotional needs of his adult, love-barren years? What right did I have to pass judgment?

At lunch I smiled at him, and it was as if heaven had opened its doors for my saddened, chastised father. The storm clouds had passed over our heads. Only a small scar remained in memory, never to be forgotten.

For a few years after that, cousin Elaine did not come to our town, even for vacations. Then the war broke out and other things became all important and life much more complicated, but that's another story.

Night Call

Skeets ran heedlessly into the night, leaving behind him the dingy, cockroach-ridden kitchen where his grandmother sat under a naked light bulb, reading *The Amsterdam News*.

He didn't care no more, he said to himself. He didn't want to see none of them, or answer their questions.

"Just tell us where you get the stuff," the officer had asked. "We won't hurt you none," he said. "You ain't a user yourself, kid, we know that," he said. "Come on, you can trust us. Nobody will ever know."

Skeets snorted with contempt at the memory. Nobody will know! As though half the precinct didn't collect payola from Big Knife, steady like, month after month.

"If you ever shoot your mouth off, kid," Big Knife's words had come hissing from between his yellowish teeth. "Remember . . . ." His lips made a smacking noise, signifying the end, as his pink, fleshy hand with carefully manicured nails reached out for Skeets's throat.

Well, they never did nab him with the stuff, not Skeets, the best of the pushers. And they never would, he'd see to that. The whole crooked dirty bunch of them. Getting paid off and then grabbing some small fish like himself to show the public they were doing something. Politics, that's what it was. He wasn't buying any of their promises to keep his ass out of jail. Thanks! For nothing!

Just because the big boss in Gracie Mansion decided to get himself reelected, the squeeze was on. Skeets hadn't been able to make a dollar all week. Not that he was that hard up—he had a couple of hundred stashed away in his mattress. He wasn't the type to throw his money around. A few games of pool, a couple of beers with his friends, a lay once in a while—that was his amusement. So far he never once had to pay for a lay, they were easy enough to come by, especially if he'd buy them a beer or take them to a show.

He didn't even like spending money on fancy clothes like some of the guys. In his business it wasn't good to look outstanding. His grandmother didn't need much; she had her social security and some-times still cleaned for the white folks when the spirit moved her, though he'd told her more than once she didn't have to no more.

Anyway, the panic had been on for over a week. The big guys were laying low and there wasn't nothing coming through. Though he wasn't starving, money wasn't coming in and Skeets was getting restless. Rumors flew thick and fast in the neighborhood—some said this thing was for real this time and nobody knew how long it would last. They didn't scare Skeets none. It would all blow over soon, he thought. It always did.

He was in this poolroom, a decent dive, where he usually stopped in once or twice a week, minding his own business, when the lieutenant from the narcotics squad sidles up to him, in front of everybody, and says:

"Hey, kid, how would you like to come down to the station with me, so as we two could have a little chat?"

Now Skeets didn't like nobody to call him "kid," him being almost twenty-two, and especially not the lieutenant. "I wouldn't, not particularly, sir," he replied, civil-like anyway, no use starting up with the cops at a time like this with the panic on.

"You don't say, boy," drawled the lieutenant, and Skeets liked that "boy" even less than the "kid," but kept his mouth buttoned up tight.

"You'd better come along, anyhow . . . ."

So naturally Skeets went.

At the station the captain got hold of him right away. First he tried to sweettalk him into giving out with the names. Skeets could see that the man with the election was getting desperate, and they needed a big arrest, bad. Well, they weren't going to get it out of him. He remembered which side his bread was buttered on. Those sons of bitches knew well enough what would happen to his hide if he talked, so it was a waste of time all around. Still he wasn't too surprised when the captain got kinda tough with him and started pushing him around a bit. It was his job, wasn't it? Only thing was, why pick on him, and him minding his own business in the poolroom? Lots of guys made bigger money on junk than he did, but no, he just happened to be handy. His luck!

When they got through knocking him around and saw there was nothing doing, they let him go.

"Let me catch you with the goods just once," the captain warned him. "You'll be sorry you ever drew breath. We'll give you such a going over you won't recognize your own mug! Release the bastard!"

That was the law for you, thought Skeets as he blinked in the neon lights out on the street. Pushing you around, just waiting for you to make a slip. He'd just about had it tonight, and no new change jingling in his pocket.

He stopped at a bar around the corner and had a shot of whiskey, he was that low.

A crinkly young-old man in an orange shirt slid onto the bar stool next to him.

"Hiya, kid. Long time no see."

This was Candle, Big Knife's right arm, who never said nothing to no purpose, as Skeets well knew.

"Had a nice session with the finest?" He gave Skeets a sharp but still playful jab in the ribs.

"Don't get it into your head to start talking none, kid. The boss is in a mighty bad temper, itchy to break somebody's bones. Yours could be as good as any. A double bourbon."

Skeets stared gloomily into his drink.

"Don't take it none too hard, kid. Soon as this blows over the boss's mood will improve, provided you're solid. Another bourbon."

Skeets just sat, his taste for drinking gone. Candle's talk could sober anybody up.

"The boss wants you to stick around," the voice droned on. "So don't get no fancy ideas to skip town or something. We'll know where to find you. Got it? Well, so long, kid."

The orange shirt slid softly off the stool and was gone.

Skeets trudged heavily up the steps of the tenement where he lived, and slammed the front door.

"That you, Skeets?" His grandmother was in the kitchen puttering around the stove.

"Yeah, it's me. Who did you think?"

He went into the bedroom and threw himself on the bed.

He had had it all right, right up to the teeth.

The cops, Big Knife, even his grandmother. What the hell did they all want from him? It wasn't fair.

"You wanna eat something, Skeets?" his grandmother poked her head in the door.

"Don't feel like nothing. Just leave me alone."

"Nothin' but liquor and women," she muttered. "It'd be enough for any man to lose his appetite. Have it your own way."

The door closed again.

He knew what he could expect.

"I'll cut you to bits," from Big Knife.

"We'll give you a nice slow death in a cozy jail," from the coppers.

Who did they think he was? Nothing?

He'd show them. He was a free man and nobody's slave. He'd had this town and the town had had him. He was going to leave and that was that. It was as good as done and nobody but the wind to chase him.

He reached under the mattress to a spot where the stuffing was coming out. Inside the hole was the reassuring touch of wrinkled bills. He counted out fifty dollars then changed his mind and put twenty-five back in his pocket, shoved the other twenty-five in an old envelope, and wrote on top:

"I'm leaving. Don't open the door to nobody."

He left the envelope on the dresser propped against a faded photograph of his mother that his grandmother insisted on leaving around. He'd never known his mother. It was small loss, he felt.

The old lady made no sign as he whizzed through the kitchen on his way out. She knew better than to bother him when he was in this mood.

His only thought now was to get out of town. The city was choking him, making him feel helpless, trapped, and afraid.

He took the subway to the suburbs, then a bus, then another bus. Soon he was walking on a well-traveled highway. A white man gave him a lift. Then another. In the morning, a black guy in a yellow station wagon stopped for him.

"Where you goin', son?"

"Anywhere."

"I'll be getting' off this road in a ways, but you're welcome to ride as long as you like. Hop in. You from this part of the country?"

"Nope."

"Talkative, ain't you? Very pretty country hereabouts. Just you open up your eyes, son."

Skeets, who until that moment had been more anxious to put distance between himself and the big town than to look at scenery, paused to gaze around carefully for the first time. They were climbing up a winding country road. Evergreens interspersed with an occasional brilliantly hued maple surrounded the road on both sides. The vegetation was so thick that in spots it almost completely obliterated their view of the sky. Green things spread in a profusion of growth on the pine-needled forest floor. Autumn was just beginning to descend on this quiet, scent-filled, and unpeopled domain.

Something familiar though long forgotten stirred in his memory.

His grandmother, holding his small hand in hers, on the way to the settlement house.

"I'm gonna register you, so as you can go to the country this summer. To camp. I've been promising myself to do it all year. So be good now, don't mess up things none."

"I don't wanna go to camp."

"It's too hot in the city, you know that."

"I like it. I can always get wet at a fire hydrant."

"Don't give me none of your lip. You're going to camp."

His grandmother was a force to be reckoned with in those days, so Skeets went to camp. The first year, then the second, the third, and so it seemed to go on for a hundred summers. By the time he was sixteen he had a job in the kitchen and did some tinkering around the camp. They treated him square enough.

In camp it was one big happy family, with everybody eating together, playing ball, putting on shows. But man, once you went back to the city things got to be as they always were before—and, Skeets was sure, always would be. He did his job and kept to himself, and no complaints. None of that phony fraternizing stuff for him. They liked him, and they were an all right bunch of guys, for white guys that is. So long as a person didn't take all their good intentions too seriously.

"What's the name of this place we're at?" he suddenly asked the driver who was giving him a lift.

"Deer Town. Why?"

"Nothing. Just that I have an uncle hereabouts, so if you'd let me off in about a mile I could walk to his place from there."

"Okay, kid. Suit yourself."

Skeets waited till the car was well out of sight, then turned unerringly into a narrow, hardly noticeable pathway on the left side of the road. He had often sneaked through there when he was in a hurry to get back to camp after his day off. He'd discovered it when he was still a camper, on one of them "nature hikes." Boy, what a laugh they were.

"What's the name of that tree, Mr. Kenneth?"

"That's an Austrian pine, very rare in this part of the country. I'm glad you noticed it, Johnny."

Who cares? Skeets thought. Could that stupid Johnny tell the difference between the latest model Cadillac and last year's Lincoln? Bet he couldn't. But Skeets could tell the year and make of any car in a split second—and he was a specialist on the expensive models. He'd have a white Cadillac to drive in one of them days, and he didn't need no Austrian pines to show him how to get one.

He had to bend low to avoid some of the overhanging branches.

Soon the outlines of cabins, grouped around a large wooden dining hall emerged from among the trees.

The main buildings of the camp were in a clearing, with a few trees shading the gentle slope that led down to the lake front. The road to the lake was paved with little stones and lined with sturdy log cabins on both sides. Most had only screens for protection, but Skeets knew that two or three had real windows, and one even had a log-burning fireplace. He headed for the director's cabin a little off to the side, with a nice kitchen and a screened porch overhanging the lake.

The camp had been closed for some weeks. No one went near it all winter. He'd be safe enough. Who would think to look for him in this place?

Breaking the handle on the porch door was child's play. The door between the porch and the cabin interior wasn't even locked.

The furniture was pushed into the middle of the room. He pushed it back against the walls. A dresser, a couch with some pillows on it, a table, and he even found a forgotten blanket. Somebody had left a doll on the floor. When he kicked it aside he saw that it had a gaping hole in the back of its head. There was a little toothpaste in the bathroom, and pots and dishes in the kitchen. The water would be turned off but there was plenty of it in the lake. He had a good hiding place all right.

Skeets stretched out on the couch. He could have gone for a sandwich and a cup of coffee. Should have thought to ask the old geezer to leave him off closer to town so as he could buy some food. But the idea of coming here had hit him so suddenly. Oh well, he'd go a bit later; there was plenty of time. He closed his eyes.

It was pitch dark when he woke up. Night had stolen upon the cabin while he was asleep, and he fumbled in his pocket for matches. Next to them he found a forgotten crumpled package of cigarettes. He took one, lit it, inhaled. It dulled his hunger. He had a few lifesavers left. That would have to do until morning. He groped along the top of the dresser. There must be candles around here somewhere; lights were always blowing out in camp. What was that? His hands rested on the familiar shape of a telephone. He lit another match.

It was the intercom. The only outside phone was in the office, way over on the other side of camp. He could just imagine using it to call the town grocery:

"This is Mr. Skeets speaking. How about sending up some salami and some rolls and some beer for my supper?"

That would be something! The outside phone was probably disconnected for the winter anyhow. But that intercom! What a pain in the neck it was. One ring for the director, two rings for the assistant director, three rings for the doctor, four rings for the head of the teenage unit, five rings . . . oh, well, he wasn't even sure he was remembering it right. The damned thing had never stopped ringing. The hush of the camp was very different from the bustle he recalled. It soothed him. He kind of liked the stillness.

In the third dresser drawer he found some candles and set one up in a small glass ashtray. Tomorrow he'd get more matches. He went out the back door. The night was mild and the dark sky full of stars. How long since he had seen stars? Years maybe. Sometimes in camp he used to look up at them and wonder what they were like. Cold as ice, a lot they cared about a crumb of humanity down below. His grandmother with her crazy notions about the heavens and goodness and power of God. Well, maybe there was a God somewhere, but there was no use on counting none on his goodness. Every man for himself, that was his motto.

He went down the stone steps toward the lake, needing no light. A gentle breeze blew through the tops of trees. Skeets sat down on the last step and lit another cigarette. Then it hit him. Why hadn't he thought of him before? He hadn't for a long time, for three years at least, ever since that day he told Jerry what he was doing . . . .

He had met Jerry down at the lake on one of his solitary walks during the last of his summers at camp. Jerry was the new head of the teenage unit. He was single, tall and spare of limb, darkhaired and athletic, with irregular rough-hewn features, about twenty-five. He was good at sports and strict with the kids, but full of jokes so that they liked and respected him. Skeets gave him credit. It was no small accomplishment to keep those teenagers in check all day and out of the bushes at night. Jerry never tried that phony equal stuff with him either, and didn't go out of his way to be more polite to a black man than was proper to be to a white one.

"Why in hell don't you put out that cigarette," Jerry said that night at the lake. "It's nothing but poison in your young lungs."

"Gotta die sometime."

"Yeah, but what's the rush? Must you take a little arsenic every day to sort of speed things up?"

Skeets grinned. That Jerry wasn't a bad guy.

That's how it began between them. Jerry taught him to play basketball even though Skeets had never touched a ball before in his life and didn't want to.

"You're scared. People always are of the things they can't do well.

Are you worried it will make you look bad? You have a good body for it and you'll see how wonderful it will feel to use it well. Come on, Skeets, play ball!"

He drew his breath in sharply, remembering the feeling of elation, of oneness with the ball as he dribbled toward the basket. His timing was perfect as he leaped up and gently banked the ball in off the backboard. There was a smattering of applause.

"Two, four, six, eight, who do we appreciate? Skeets! Skeets! Skeets!" came the staccato voices of the yelling teenagers. He basked for a brief spell in the sunshine of that long since spent acclaim.

"What are you going to do with yourself when the summer's over?" That was Jerry, getting on his back again after the game, with Skeets still wiping the sweat off his face and arms.

"Why don't you go back to high school, try to finish this time, maybe go on to college. You can't get far without an education."

"I hate school."

"Same story as with basketball. You never tried to do well in school, that's why. I'll get you some tutoring. Think about it, will you?"

He thought about it. In September, Jerry went back to a job in a settlement house. At night he still took some graduate courses. He had a little room with a kitchenette near the college, and when Skeets came to visit him there he often cooked supper for both of them.

One night he nudged him again.

"You want other people to respect you, Skeets, right? How are they going to when you don't respect yourself? So how about it? You going back to school?"

So Skeets went back to school. With Jerry's tutoring he lasted it out almost a whole year, and even got better than just passing grades.

It was getting chilly at the lake shore and Skeets, his cigarette out, ground it into the earth with the heel of his foot.

Anyhow, he had this fight in the playground with an Italian kid who called him a nigger. He would have killed the son of a bitch if two teachers hadn't separated them. Skeets was way over age to be in high school. They had only taken him back in the first place on Jerry's word and on his promise that he'd keep his hands off the younger kids. So he was out, finished.

He didn't go near Jerry's room for weeks. He wasn't around his own house much but his grandmother told him that Jerry had been in, trying to see him. Skeets didn't feel like talking about it. What the hell was the use?

Then he got this job in a skirt factory for thirty-five bucks a week and the boss wanting blood. After that he drove a truck, worked in a supermarket sweeping floors, had one or two other lousy jobs. He didn't like the hours or the pay or the way they talked to him. He went back to the poolroom and the corner tavern, and when Big Knife offered him a deal, he took it.

Big Knife was a big man. The work was easy enough, the money good. He didn't have to take no crap from nobody.

"One of my boys is as good as another. Black or white, makes no difference to me. You do your job, I treat you right."

Skeets got up, ambled up the hill toward the cabin. He wandered a little farther up the road to the ball field. They never did keep that field in good repair. Always saying it was bad for the kids to indulge in too much competition in sports. Except for Jerry. Boy, did that guy believe in ball playing! Skeets peeked into the arts and crafts hall, where scraps of bright paper and multicolored felt still littered the tables and chairs. It was no use trying not to think about that last time with Jerry.

Jerry had come down to the poolroom, looking for him.

"What's wrong, Skeets? Why haven't you called or been to see me?"

"Had no time. Been working and busy like, you know."

"Come on don't give me that. What's the real reason?"

"I told you, I'm working."

"Doing what?"

"Well, I got me a little business, I do all right."

"What kind of business?"

Okay, if he was going to be that nosy, he would let him have it. He probably suspected anyhow.

"Selling junk."

Jerry recoiled visibly.

"You? A pusher?"

"Yeah."

"Are you on the stuff yourself?"

"Who me? I ain't that stupid."

He knew that his bad English would annoy Jerry.

"Then it's just for money."

"Yep. What did you think it was for? If the suckers want it, I got it."

Jerry's face seemed constricted with pain. Even his lips went white.

"I'll tell you what I think," he said very slowly. "To me, a pusher is the lowest form of life. He's no better than a murderer. He deserves to be shot."

He turned away abruptly. Skeets, frozen and still, saw Jerry's back disappear through the door.

The lowest form of life, he thought now in the silence of the camp. Maybe he was, though he'd met a few others who could give him a push where being low was concerned. Anyhow, Jerry shouldn't have said that. He sauntered back to the cabin and went to bed.

The ringing of the telephone woke him from a deep sleep. It took a few seconds before he quite realized where he was, the veils of sleep unraveling slowly. But the phone kept ringing, and he shook himself awake enough to count the rings.

One for the director, two for the assistant director, three for the doctor, four . . . . He was about to reach for the receiver with a shaking hand, when he halted. The instrument stopped dead after the fifth ring.

It was the middle of autumn and there was no one but himself in the camp. The intercom could not have been ringing. Unless there was someone hiding amid the dark shadows outside his cabin. He pushed a table against the front door, the couch against the porch door, then cautiously raised one of the curtains to peer out, straining to hear the sound of footsteps. Last evening's friendly darkness could now contain an enemy. The trees might be sheltering a sinister figure that could threaten his life.

All was deadly still as Skeets kept up his watch. Could Big Knife have had him traced this soon? Or maybe it was the police? He dared not move, except to feel for the knife in his pocket. Whoever the intruder was, Skeets was prepared.

In the early dawn his panic subsided. The place seemed deserted and peaceful. He ventured out through the back porch, walking stealthily like a cat, searching cautiously at first, then with greater confidence. There wasn't a sign of a human presence.

Reassured, he got his few things together. He was hungry as a hog. Followed or not, it was time for him to get on. Wasn't the whole wide world open to him? Like the South, maybe? That was a laugh! Chicago? It was like New York, except he knew nobody there. In New York he'd get along. Hadn't he always? Big Knife would get over his short absence, he'd know Skeets hadn't squealed. As for the cops, the panic would probably be over soon and they wouldn't be so nervous no more.

As he walked along the path through the woods toward the highway, Skeets thought back to the telephone ringing in the night. Who could it have been? Maybe he had been dreaming after all. But he could have sworn!

It must have been a dream, he decided. And him thinking it was Big Knife on the intercom!

He hailed a passing motorist bound for the city.

"Night Call," published in the collection The Invisible Passage *in 1969, is loosely based on the young men with whom my husband, a social worker, worked in Harlem and on Manhattan's Lower East Side.*

Public and Private

Tommy Isn't One
of My Heroes

To the Editor:

As a child of a family of political dissenters who often saw the inside of jails in pre-World War II Poland, and a writer, I tend to view literature produced by cons and ex-cons with special sympathy. In that spirit I read Kay Boyle's enthusiastic appraisal of Tommy Trantino's *Lock the Lock* (Alfred A. Knopf) under your BOOKS, April 18–20. Ms. Boyle makes much of how Trantino, now serving a life sentence in Rahway, N.J., could teach her and her writing students about "crying out his life like music." Ms. Boyle then takes us to page ninety-four of the book where Trantino gives himself up to the New York police following the murder of two cops in the Angel Bar. He had been too drunk, it is claimed, to know what had happened, and the shots that killed did not come from his gun. There is a quoted paragraph from Trantino's deposition, well written in a staccato style. When I came to the words "Frank gets the other cop and frisks him . . . ." etc., I experienced a sudden illumination that placed the piece in its proper focus.

"Frank" is undoubtedly Frankie F. (it would be too much to expect another case so identical). Angel Tavern was in Lodi, New Jersey. The case was notorious. Who was Frank F.? Please bear with me if I take you back some years. My husband was one of New York City's early so-called "street youth workers." He was unusually successful. Throughout his long association with private agencies in Harlem and on the Lower East Side of Manhattan he developed both genuine friendship and a mutual respect with members of some of the most "hostile" youth gangs. This was in their heyday, before drugs appeared heavily on the scene to turn anger into quiet desperation.

In all the years in this kind of work he met only one young person he considered thoroughly amoral—Frank F. Frank was unsalvageable because he was criminally insane. He was a cheap hood who terrorized the neighborhood—his hatred of minorities was pathological. To comprehend it was to be in a cellar club with a group of frightened Puerto Rican and black youngsters while Frank raged in the gutter, blasting garbage cans against the club's windows, sputtering curses, shooting at random. (Frank F. was the organizer of bloody gang wars against black and Puerto Rican youth who were moving into the Lower East Side.) It was to see the face of an older fellow who came to their rescue reduced to a bloody pulp beneath Frank's heels. It was to watch his oft-beaten and abused young wife make her frequent charges to the police. It was to identify the bodies of his "enemies" fished out of the East River.

Rumor had it that his older brothers had connections with top gangsters (Frank seemed to get off with relatively light sentences), and everyone was afraid to tackle him. Finally a judge ordered Frank to remove his presence from the Lower East Side. When sometime later he went on a rampage in a Lodi bar accompanied by a friend (Tommy Trantino?) and killing two policemen, he was wanted on a murder rap and on charges of beating another police officer. Although the papers failed to report it, he had first forced the two policemen to undress and perform what the law termed "unnatural acts" before they died. A couple of days later the cops got a tip that Frank F. was holed up in a sleazy Manhattan hotel. They kicked in the door, went in, guns blazing. It was a violent end to a violent life, and the reason for Trantino's surrender.

Now that we have an outline of the story we can return to our reviewer. Ms. Boyle is a critic of the establishment, and Trantino's book she feels "exposes our times." Ipso facto, that makes of him a legitimate critical voice, worthy of an audience. The implication is inserted—through the mouth of a student in a writing class and a quotation from Trantino's mother—that he is a "genius." Ms. Boyle even sees fit to include him in the illustrious company of social moralizers—Malraux, Richard Wright, Dostoyevsky, Solzhenitsyn, and Koestler—an odious comparison.

Which brings me to the point: How far afield can the best of us stumble in our opposition to the ugliness and injustice of our environment? Genius, indeed, but what a perverted one! A quoted paragraph about his third grade teacher, the atom bomb, and the Russians constitutes no absolution. To me it is pure bullshit, a copout by a superb con artist. So what if our society is full of jingoism? Is this enough to send a genius (or anybody) into the companionable arms of a Frankie F.?

Trantino's "music" is sour. My guru he can never be, and if I am to march, it will have to be to a different drummer.

Sincerely yours,

Irena P. Narell

Oakland

"Tommy Isn't One of My Heroes" a letter published in the Pacific Sun *in Marin County, was in response to an elaborate article by Kay Boyle in a previous issue of the paper. I knew too many people who attributed idealistic motives to hardened criminals, worked with them, and got badly burned.*

Introduction to:
My Beloved is Mine

The prophets often used the metaphor of marital love to describe the relationship between Israel and God. Love between a man and a woman culminating in marriage and the establishment of a home is a central theme in Jewish tradition.

The *Song of Songs,* a peerless anthology of love poems treasured by the Jews, is heavily allegorical. In it the people of Israel and God are posed in the guise of a woman and her beloved. This hidden meaning prompted the great Rabbi Akiba to uphold the right of the *Song of Songs* to a place in the scriptures. ". . . for all the *Writings* are Holy, but the *Song of Songs* is the Holy of Holies," said Akiba.

No formal description of the wedding ceremony exists in the Bible, save the simple act of living together: "And Isaac brought her into his mother Sarah's tent, and took Rebekah, and she became his wife and he loved her . . . ." (Genesis 24:67). Ritual associated with marriage evolved during the rabbinical period of Jewish history. The Hebrew word for marriage is *kiddushin* or sanctification. Each bride and groom perpetuate, through the act of matrimony, the existence of the Jewish people and the values represented by Judaism. Yet the ancient sages cautioned that no human endeavor is as significant or as fraught with danger—for only a good marriage can bring "joy, blessing, goodness . . . Torah, protection, and peace."

The *ketubbah,* a marriage contract stating a man's obligations as a husband and those incumbent upon him in case of death or divorce, dates back to ancient Judea, and is still a requirement in traditional ceremonies. The husband's duties to provide for his wife's material needs are clearly defined. Moreover, according to custom he is to "love her as himself but honor her more than himself."

Traditionally, a wife's part is of paramount importance. She is not to be looked upon solely as a necessary partner for fulfilling the commandment "to be fruitful and multiply," nor merely as a man's companion. She complements her husband, and, as the rabbis say, "a wifeless man is a deficient man." A wife should be both "tended and cherished." Her praises are sung in the Jewish household at the beginning of each Sabbath eve.

The home has played a key role in the life of the Jewish people for centuries. The rites and ceremonies performed there made it as significant a center of religion as the synagogue. Thus the woman who presided over the household became the bearer of Jewish tradition. The figure of the devoted Jewish wife and mother has been a persistent theme in Jewish folklore.

Rachel, the wife of Rabbi Akiba, symbolizes the most desirable traits attributed to women in Jewish folk history. She left a comfortable home for the love of an unlettered, humble shepherd. She discerned the gleam of intellect beneath a rough exterior and encouraged his studies, refusing to let him quit. To help him, she took a job outside the home. She suffered separation, poverty, and deprivation so that her husband might become a wise rabbi, devoted to learning, social justice, and the service of God. Her exemplary life is illustrated by the following story:

One day the sages gathered in Bene Berak and asked among themselves: "What is true wealth?" Tarfon, the rich landowner, replied: "The possession of a hundred vineyards and a hundred slaves to work them." Young Meir, Akiba's disciple, said: "Contentment with one's riches." Akiba was the last to speak. "A wife who is beautiful in her deeds," was his reply—surely an apt description of Rachel.

The ideal Jewish home was to be permeated by the lofty precepts of parental responsibility and filial devotion, accompanied by mutual love—love between husband and wife, parents and children. Through dowry and wedding gifts, many of them symbols of tradition, the woman created and embellished the family's physical surroundings. Throughout the ages, wives and mothers were seen as a source of strength and stability for the entire family, quite in contrast with the distorted image presented by modern Jewish novelists.

Nor has the twentieth-century woman lagged behind our folkloric heroines. This era has produced Henrietta Szold, Hannah Senesh, Anne Frank, Golda Meir, and so many others who transcended family obligations, translating them into love and sacrifice for humanity. They have embraced the affirmation of life and sensitivity to feelings in the face of adversity and even death. They have left their mark upon the entire world.

On the occasion of the twentieth anniversary of the Judah L. Magnes Museum, the Women's Guild celebrates the significance of the Jewish woman. The show features some of the infinite variety of Jewish custom through art and ceremonial objects associated with the

wedding and the home. Rich in Sephardic heritage, the Museum collections enable us for the first time to share these less well-known
treasures with a wider audience.

*This introduction to the J. L. Magnes Museum Catalogue for "My
Beloved is Mine," in 1982, is included because it contains some of my
feelings about Jewish tradition and the role of women in Jewish history.*

Relationship

He was;
My father and my mother,
My sister and my brother,
My lover, my companion, my protector,
And above all, my best friend—

From the moment we met
He—stricken by a "thunderbolt"—
Never wavered in his love for me,
Tall, dark, and handsome,
He was loyal to all he cared for,
To his principles, his friends,
Intensely loyal to me,
He was unseduceable and incorruptible,

He had a great heart that
Embraced me, his children,
His grandchildren, other people's children,
His fellow Jews, all suffering humanity,
Dynamic and adventurous,
A maverick, an original,
He was capable of righteous anger,

Beneath a deceivingly tough exterior,
He was passionate and sentimental,
Intelligent, sometimes brilliant—
Deeply interested in the present
And in history,
Innovative, opinionated, inexhaustibly energetic,
Argumentative and controversial,
A fierce debater and a teller of terrific jokes—

A supremely talented athlete,
A college basketball star,
He was not vain, nor selfish,
Nor self-absorbed,
He was fearless—a champion

Of unpopular causes.
He had no use for power plays or for fools,

A fanatic about promptness,
He had a sly wit, an infectious smile,
A fabulous cook, he baked splendid bread,
And an "outrageous" cheesecake,
He played "scientific" blackjack to "beat the Mafia"—

He was good to talk to,
Responsive to my feelings,
My interests in art and writing,
Physically strong,
Emotionally strong,
An eternal optimist,
He tried to shield me from pain—

He cared about important things,
Not money, not ambition,
Not power—but about people, laughter,
Intellectual stimulation, the give and take
Of political controversy,
Performance in sports—especially tennis and basketball,
Trinidadian steel band music,
Old Caruso and Paul Robeson records, Spanish cantos,
But most of all, about
Doing the right thing—

He forgave my trespasses, overlooked
My inadequacies,
My stumbling,
He tried to teach me,
That my ambitions, my unhappiness,
My frustrations, and
Sometimes my depression,
Could be assuaged and curtailed,
If I too paid less attention to career,
Achievement and literary fame,
And more to being a good person—
And doing what I could for others,

And to the genuine love
With which he surrounded me,—

He was courageous to the
Point of recklessness when it
Came to what he believed to be right,
He was always there for me,
And when dying—his major concern
Was still for me—he grieved that
He would not be there when I needed him—

His courage never failed him,
Not even at the end,
He orchestrated his death with gallantry,
As he did his life—

The gods were cruel—
I mourn for all he has had to forego,
I miss him, I miss his humor,
The sound of his laughter,
His strength, the sharing of ideas, my hand in his,
And his arms around me,

My heart is still sore,
But it is also expanding
To include others—
To whom I now can be
A real friend,
A closer friend,
A better friend,
And I am trying
To go on with my life,
Even if I falter,
To regain my concern for the world,
The gift of laughter, and
Writing,
And perhaps, only perhaps,
Somewhere, sometime,
To care for someone again—

July 1992